HIGHER RESOLUTION VS GEOPOLITICAL RISKS

HIGHER RESOLUTION VS GEOPOLITICAL RISKS

BY NICOLAS ISMAEL

Nicolas Ismael
Higher Resolution Vs Geopolitical Risks

Published by BooxAI
1500 Getaway Blvd, Boynton Beach, FL
ISBN: 978-965-578-913-3

BooX AI

As someone barely turning seventy, but still feeling and appearing very hairless. It would remain an ineffable and everlasting error on my part if first aboard, I let pass by this golden opportunity to not say thank you to President Donald Trump for inspiring me and also serving as compass for a job well done. Thank you again, because it is thanks to you that I was able to draw my inspiration source to write this book.

Therefore, as I pointed out above, being a sexagenarian, I have been inspired by you, President Trump when through one of your speeches regarding age factors which are not supposed excuses preventing Joe Biden from knowing how to lead well.

You said from your experience, you have often gotten in touch with many people, more especially senior citizens who at such a similar age have become opulent and achieved many things that they were not be able to accomplish during their entire youth. So, using the age issue is just an excuse on Biden's part because he knows what he's doing. Thus. It's well planned and intentioned on his part.

Besides, is there not a great writer formulating:

Age often leads to the reason?

Finally, when you formulated these words of encouragement and hope towards the senior citizens to never lose confidence and faith, such wonderful thoughts went straight to my mind to encourage me moving forward to write and relate this esthetic political story regarding your entire life style.

And I'm proud of sharing it with all my fellow Americans.

TABLE OF CONTENTS

I'M NICOLAS ISMAEL

Since I have known the day, it would appear that I had already a microphone in my mouth, leading me to dedicate myself to the profession of journalism as a natural versatile in this field. Unfortunately, it is quite regrettable that I was born and raised in a dictatorial country considered a pure Banana Republic, which is quite incomparable and immeasurable to the one: The country of dreams and freedom, which is the United States of America.

Contrary to what so many people of several other countries believe, namely, it is a country where racism, prejudice of all kinds, and barriers of race always fill up and spill oil between people of different nationalities who live in this said country.

Because of my knowledge, I did acquire a certain good sense which allows me to appeal to conscience and the common sense of reason to detect the truth from the falsehood. Therefore, there still exists a whole feud and avalanche of people who will not be of the same mind and notice because the faculty of knowledge will always be lacking in them.

As a result, they only believe in what they see and hear. Yet, this belief, once misinterpreted and miscalculated, has become erroneous, while oftentimes transformed into a myth and taboo, incarcerating in the mentality of people who believe in it as being well-digestive, while indelible and difficult to be forgotten and pushed aside. It's so true that they use it every 4 years during the electoral period to make people believe that Donald Trump has only one objective in mind, that of implementing and practicing the policy of racism in this country.

For those, as noted above, possessing a certain faculty of knowledge and being accustomed to those kinds of behaviors of hidden sense, it is no longer a secret that it is and remains a clever innate stratagem used by the Democratic party every 4 years in matters of any elections, more specifically the presidential ones, to convince people with hollow heads and ant minds considered as wild ducks to go to the polls in doves and droves to cast ballots in their favor.

However, such clever tactics practiced by the political party in question are not new today! This has always existed for years! Having often succeeded wonderfully, they overjoyed it with joy except when the situation of the country is ultra crucial under their leadership as it was the case in 1980 and also currently speaking.

Praise the Lord, this time, the technology is very advanced without forgetting the social media with a minority layer that have worked tirelessly to bring out the hidden meaning of history, allowing people to become aware because they are often the main victimized.

However, what many people, perhaps through ignorance or malice, fail to understand is that: Just like the Democrats, numerous so-called "former collaborators" who were supposedly to be considered allies and support structures of President Donald Trump, not only betrayed, but also, even today, they continue to use these same expressions of shenanigans to blast the latter and attempt by all possible ways to put him in a similar basket of dirty work and policy of letting go practiced by President Joe Biden, where avant-garde factor, such as diplomacy, economy, security, and justice shine wonderfully in abstention among whom, we would like to list in big headlines - Chris Christie, Governor R. DeSantis, and more precisely Nikki Haley, the former ambassador of President Donald Trump who once qualified her former boss as the best and greatest president of the United States, while actually standing on the cross to shoot red balls at him and mistreat him in words with unfounded and unreal criticism concerning China and inflation during debates and campaigns.

But, why these critical and hurtful interlocutors responsible for the debates never had the decency to ask Nikki Haley: Are you aware that China's Covid-19 cost the United States a colossal amount of 6.6 trillion dollars?

Perhaps, which with no doubt did not attract the attention of the three so-called famous hosts of the 4th republican presidential primary debate!

Now the question to ask: Was it a weakness or partiality on the part of these interlocutors for at least not even one of them did not follow the erroneous response of Nikki Haley in the circumstances?

In any case, what we know for sure is something that is repeated and reiterated.

Remember the 2020 debate between President Trump and former Vice-President Biden led by the so-called "moderator-conservator" Chris Wallace? This ultra-important question of the discovery of Hunter Biden's Laptop was revealed by President Trump who asked Biden to shed light on such a scandal, which represents a great danger in sign of treason for the nation!

Unfortunately, an important and interesting subject which should have made headlines news for the delectation and comprehension of many million American voters was categorically refused by this famous Chris Wallace who acted in Master and Lord to impose his Vero by telling President Donald Trump that: Receiving money from China and the discovery of transactional shenanigans found on Hunter's Laptop have nothing to see with foreign affairs, it's no longer a question and subject of the debate tonight MISTER THE PRESIDENT!

Now, let's return to our fundamental subject.

Speaking of discrimination and racism, we would say that it's a question of propaganda to put the United States into such a basket of spoiled oranges, not to say, an avilishing and embarrassing situation. Why not an aberration?

To testify in it, being an excellent speaker knowing what speaking means, if I had been born in the United States, I would never experience financial difficulties in my daily life. Then, just a little anecdote. One day, my ex-wife looked at me blankly and said to me: "Nick, you're a well-respected broadcaster. You speak four languages! Why are you poor? Sean Hannity only speaks English!"

Segundo, Carine Jean Pierre, the new revelation appointed by Kamala for rendered services during the election period of 2020, she's not ugly like me to scare you, but she doesn't have an angelic beauty either! Just like the superstar, Sean Hannity, only speaks English! Perhaps a little Creole, too! Therefore, it would not be surprising if we approach her in this language and then she turned a deaf ear and pretended not to understand! But don't ask me why because the heart has its reasons that reason itself does not know!

Without going any further, did she ever answer the questions of the African journalist? Until the latter, finally must have understood that his presence in this confines of the press conference would appear and mean embarrassment for Madame the Lecturer, CJP, the first of everything as she declared it when she took investiture? So, is Donald Trump the only Shark in the red sea that eats and goes it alone!? Isn't it?

If this is by accident you would say so, cut it off right away!! Give us a break! Then, despite all, these shortcomings, it means tangible proof that the USA is far from being qualified as a country full of racism and prejudice, because Madame CJP is one of the highest-paid figures in this country of dreams. Yet, this bad qualification to which the

USA is attributed, is not meaningful at all! Why can it be? It's really true that CJP is already a multimillionaire in a short period of time?! Why is it often considered racist by the same left quite opulent? Actually, do not be so worried. The cat is out of the bag! Her salary is evaluated at 180,000 US greens a year, while her net worth has already peaked up 10 million US$.

So, once again, give us a break to repeat after the great Octogenarian French Chef de Cuisine, Mr. GASTON, namely: "Everything they say about the USA is Bias and nonsense critics. They are arch false! They are real hypocrites because they know for sure that the USA is unique and true in everything!"

To back up and extend Gaston's opinion, this country by excellence, looks like a kind of unlimited international canal or mouth, into which all the rivers of the world flow? Can't we see crystal clear that under the Biden administration, already, more than 10 million immigrants left their country to come to live in the USA? Why didn't they go to Russia, China, France, or the UK? Something might be cooking better for them over here! For this particular reason, speculating that way about the USA, is just a pure calumny which has nothing to do with the reality of the facts. So, let's put this segment aside for now and let's come back to me personally.

Although a Broadcaster, who loves to write and comment on events, it was never my intention to write about politics given my experience in this area which I consider to be a dirty job.

However, being a Radio personality also means that you're an educator. You cannot act like a selfish person as other people are often mistaken for not being able to recognize the true color of the rainbow to question mother nature: What exactly is it about?

Just as we often say, if you see something, say something, I believe, as a citizen of the United States, I must be able to contribute my share to this country in question. In this context, seeing in Trump a real victim of the system, I have taken a final decision to write this book. Then, I say to myself, if beyond had provided me with such an inspiration, it is quite necessary to seize the opportunity to shed the light for the full comprehension of those whose knowledge about politics is limited, not to say empty.

Donald Trump is the one inspiring me to write this book in order to educate people about what they don't know. If passing through this trajectory, people are convinced, I would be proud and delighted with joy for not only speculating about JFK's theory as many other caressing hypocrites do, but also well applying it, this theory, namely: "Don't ask what your country can do for you, preferably, ask what you can do for your country."

In this sense, Higher Resolution VS Geopolitical risks already meets this theoretical formula.

Nevertheless, we are not the only ones to accomplish this duty. As pointed out above, so many black and Latinos media have already converted themselves as true architects of people's future destiny to concretize such a wonderful mission in the circumstances.

As a result, they have already reaped the expected fruits because the number grows increasing concerning blacks and Latinos who are ready to address the issue to those corrupt oligarchs, namely: don't tell us what you're going to do for the low income and poor retired senior citizens including our veterans! Preferably, tell us what you already did for us 4 years ago!

Furthermore, Ukraine, during more than two years of this war period with Russia is better rated than our senior citizens living in the heart of the country by receiving hundreds of billions US$ coming directly from the sweat of our taxpayers while the latter only lives from hand to mouth. Every day.

The proof is so great that the average salary for Ukrainians in full period of war in 2022 was evaluated at 421 US$. However, since May 2023, Ukrainians, despite having become a devastated and deserted country, benefited from an exorbitant increase of salary estimated at 25.2% to go from 421 to 521 American dollars. While on our side, acting as good Samaritans, towards others to neglect and put aside our Seniors, the latter had to wait until January 1st, 2024, to receive a small piece of increase estimated at only 3.2% of which we shall elaborate further.

So, begins this page of history dedicated to Donald J. Trump, which is a completely fair and contemporary story based on reliable statistics and the reality of the facts, making us differentiate our real friends from our notorious enemies.

Higher Resolution VS Geopolitical Risks, is a work which will serve as a reference to permit us to walk by the head, not by the tail. Also, a book which permits you to look these blatant liars in the eye and tell them, just like you, we are also educated to no longer accept flattering words and false promises in favor of words of honor and saving blessings.

Thus, talking about flattering and false promises, that leads us to go back to the ancient to make us understand and believe that since the beginning there was always love.

Far from being a theologian or fervent faithful of Christianity to do the religious education of anyone, one should be inclined to believe that when God created the world, He had us at first in His mind as human beings. Thus, creating us as such was not merely an exercise and dominance in His might, but essentially an act of love. This is a psychoanalysis and faith based on the fact which is not quite limited. All this is just to say that love is everywhere! It is found through music, politics, profession, and more specifically through erotic relationships between humans. This is also to explain that the same sentiment of love represents an avant-garde factor needed to function well in daily life. Nevertheless, this indispensable and irrefutable factor failed President Donald Trump, who was surrounded by several so-called partisans with the fox's faces who, either by jealousy or personal ambitions, instead of loving Trump and embracing with heart and open arms his logical policy of visibility furthering the pride and well-being of this country, they preferred to hate him to death.

As a result, although his firm determination was to leave us a country solid, correct, and prosperous, they, for the most part, acted in schemes to collapse him. Fortunately, not being alone, the power of divinity permits the American people to recognize in Trump a true Americano-Phile whose love for this country is quite incomparable and that everyone must be aware of it. So, because of this gratefulness, today, we are faced with a proven fact, namely: Donald Trump has become the most popular leader in the world. With an incredible and disproportionate popularity, the 195 countries existing through the planet don't hesitate to hit the deadlines with Donald Trump all fired up who, although the obstacles endured, is not only popular in all American territories but also a thorn in the leg for the Biden administration, which has sworn to do everything in its power to block the way for President Donald Trump to return to the White House on January 20, 2025. So, this biblical passage is just a reminder to Donald Trump to make him understand that since the world was the world, love has always existed. We cannot truly live together and lead well without love for one another. You must love the one who loves you. It is a sacred message. Even when we often say that past mistakes remain in the past, we must think about the future. However, we must avoid making the same mistakes of the past! With this in mind, we believe that President Trump has indeed admitted that he was not well impressed by the politicians in Washington. But as for today, he said: "I have learned my political lessons and taken notes of that."

As a simple author, but not an advisor, even if it would be a nonprofit, I would never arrogate to myself the right to propose, let alone impose a presidential cabinet on Donald Trump. But as someone with a great preference for the latter, just as you will read further in the immigration area, I would only suggest this time a cabinet that has people who like Trump and also competent and serious compatriots aware and who are well-rounded and well-trained in matters of pure love for the USA and good governance.

In this context, this tedious thought from JFK always

comes to my mind, namely: try never to ask what the country can do for you, but preferably, what you can offer to your country. Of course, President Trump is neither omnipotent nor omnipresent to know everything, but someone else seeing his clear and real vision for the country can easily advise him to make good choices for successful governance. Therefore, helping in this sense is simply applying this famous theory of JFK's, which is a good option for the advancement of the United States.

What about a mixed and diversified government which puts water in the wine of the troublemakers from the rainy camp? Also, a reliable and conscientious government making Trump a leader, breaking records in the history of the United States?

Here is the composition of a government of public safety which will make President Donald Trump, just before his departure for the East, (beyond) the main thinker not only for the Republican party but also for the country as a whole!

1)As Vice President. Senator Tim Scott from South Carolina.

2)Tucker Carlson, Secretary of States.

3)Senator Ted Cruz, DOJ.

4)Tulsi Gabbard Secretary of Defense.

5)Governor Kristi Noem, Secretary of Communication..

6)Congressman Byron Donalds Homeland security.

7)Vivek Ramaswamy , Treasurer.

8)Dr. Mehmet Oz , secretary of health.

9)MARK LEVIN, SPECIAL COLLABORATOR-ADVISOR.

10)GOV. MIKE HUKABEE . SPECIALCOL- LABORATOR- ADVISOR.

11)Newt Gingrich, Very special Adviser or Press Secretary.

12)BETSY DEVOS,

11) Ben Carlson

13 Scott Fruit, all of these Three would be recalled to

return to their respective positions for having served well during President Trump's 4 years in power.

Therefore, even when man in general is metamorphic, at least we could give a certain credit to the people mentioned above and have a little confidence in them for having always had very good cordial relations with President Donald Trump in the past and still today. Then, let's hope that they always stay faithful to President Donald Trump, contrary to Nikki Haley, Governor DeSantis, Barr, Pompeo, and Pence, not knowing that one must never forget the hand that fed you. Also, never destroy the bridge that allowed you to cross the river.

It should be noted that, upon entering into consultations with more than 10 minority media which are quite Trumpets IN RED, to find out their opinion and reaction concerning such a cabinet proposal with regard to the next president of the United States, Donald Trump, they are all delighted with it, except for a few small doubts about the well-articulated Congresswoman Tulsi Gabbard, our intellect wise man, Newt Gingrich, and Governor Kristie Noem.

So, as for Kristie, I had to clarify that it is not Big Chris, enemy number one of President Trump. By the way, certain media which do not know how to establish the difference between sweet hypocritical words and those coming out from the heart, already tend to give Chris Christie credits for not agreeing with Colorado's Judges to take Trump off the ballots and disqualify him from participating in the primary election in this said state. However, what the media in play doesn't figure out is that if Chris was really born again, just like VIVEK R., he should say, not only I disagree with Colorado, but also for the respect of our democratic system and our voters, I decide to not participate as long as the Judge's decision is not overturned and remains firm. At this time, we would take into consideration such a declaration from the ex, desperate and defrocked governor. Otherwise, it's pure words, but not action.

Overall, let's go back to our topic. It's not quite serious at all! On the contrary, they think that the formation of a

Cabinet with the caliber of these very reliable professionals and sincere personalities well imbued with the program of Americanism started by President Donald Trump which is without any doubt will allow him to score big for the country during his 4 next years in office, which will also serve as an example to the country to never return to the fraudulent promises of the great oligarchic eaters and country sellers.

Referring ourselves to several crises to which the United States is currently facing, Trump might be the only solution for a great relief. Many are those who have a good memory to remember that under Trump's leadership, the economy, the inflation, and the weakness were not the way they actually are. This is the opinion of an absolute majority who said: When Trump was in power, daily life was not so expensive. Our value and strength were not threatened and underestimated compared to our opponents in the East. But despite all, that did not prevent the left from being victorious without danger and triumph without glory in 2020.

Therefore, it is better for MAGA to lose a fight with honor rather than to win a victory in dishonor, which later will tarnish the image of a superpower country like ours, worldwide speaking to transform it into a Banana Republic that only Donald Trump can come back to heal. In the circumstances, let's pray to God because under our famous octogenarian Joe Biden, stress keeps on running rampant in the USA. Please Lord reveal to our nation your unfailing love in this time of uncertainty. Dear Lord, Just like Israel, many consider the United States as being supposed a sacred and blessed land which is currently going through an acute crisis of all kinds and almost hypothetical to notorious enemies, which demands quick guidance and protection from you, Father of the Universe!

Dear Lord, if we always say we believe in you! This explains that you will always be there to guide us, protect our marvelous nation and snatch its freedom from the hands of notorious enemies, especially China which since 2021, according to the Department of Agriculture, has already acquired a total of 393,935 acres of land in the United

States which is evaluated at half the size of New York City. Do not forget also that statistics issued by the governor of South Dakota, Kristie Noem, reveal that 86% of the medical resources of the country are provided by China. What a crucial dependency! Given Lord how the abomination in our society considerably grows, and that also with inflation which surpasses its limits, that envelopes us lately into a trajectory of a dead end. Therefore, we see ourselves in front of an overwhelming crisis in the country we all love and cherish. Do we still have one last chance to save our nation God? When we see how China, Russia, several African countries, even Arab ones seem to build a block of coalition through so-called get-together to collapse the United States as well as one of its main allies, Israel like the Berlin wall. And what about repeated threats against Taiwan, more recently, against Israel as mentioned above which is our most important partner in the Middle East? Furthermore, what to say about Cuba located about 100 miles from our Floridian Coast for which China seems to already retain a clear vision to woo in order to be closer to spy better on us? What a dangerous task!

As Donald Trump would say: "The alarm bell has already announced the color." In this current context, our country, as the leader of the world, has a great need for a serious and competent leader. Someone capable of clearly and firmly speaking, with his mind and being very respected. In this optic, given this turn and magnitude of the perilous phase of these conflicts and balance of power has just taken, to avoid the worst, we must have a unique option, that of calling: Prevention is better than cure.

Didn't Donald Trump already concretize all that during his four years in power? Didn't he make it crystal clear before his international opponents that the United States is not looking to provoke any adversary? Therefore, we will not tolerate any interference on our territory as well as that of our allies; especially, since behind the mountains, there stand other mountain ranges even higher than those of the previous ones. And all this is to let them know that we also got what you got!

Therefore, to testify, through all those years, more than fifty by extension, presidents representing the United States, the latter had always declined to officially recognize Jerusalem as Israel's capital. In fact, despite this tight collaboration and wonderful relationship between these two countries, this topic of putting up to date the recognition of Jerusalem as the capital of Israel was not taken into consideration to be the main priority on the negotiation table.

They all, for some reason that the reason itself would not know, ignored it. But today, because of Donald Trump's leadership and vision for Israel, he masterfully and finally managed to change the phase of supposedly complicated things dating back half a century. A change of policy that opened the door, which was a big challenge for many anterior presidents of the United States dating for a period of, as mentioned above, half a century, that of finally acknowledge the obvious that Jerusalem is the capital of Israel.

And this, in the eyes of all Iran-Hamas who had no other option than that of turning a deaf ear and playing blindfold to accept the fact because Trump does play game! Reacting otherwise would probably make Trump hit not only the game but also all these players in rebellions! It was not without reason, instead of reaction, we observed a silence of CATHEDRAL and CEMETERY silence on the side of Israel's enemies from then on contrary to currently where Israel has just been surprisingly and violently attacked by those theorists.

But sometimes, what's even worse is that in those kinds of political situations, our adversary leaders have often found the blessing of our own oligarchs and government's members to allow them free access to act safely without fear and without firing a shot. Thus, it was not a surprise and secret to discover underground that several left-wing activists wore the uniform of congressmen camp in crossfire to blame Israel for this barbarous act and deadly attack of terrorism. Without going further, everyone knew that after China's Covid19,

Iran was totally broken! Where did they find money to support Russia with drones and finance Hamas?

In this context, American people's memory does not fail to remember that people without memory are people without a future. That's why, in sign of recognition, they have chosen to work everlastingly with Donald Trump to give America its last chance, making it GREAT again.

Apart from that, don't you know that the barbecue was in the spotlight at the White House while Israel was on fire under this attack orchestrated by Palestinian-Iraqi terrorists? But such a weak and late performance by President Biden should not surprise us when we look back at 9/11! Where was he, this famous senator from Delaware then? He was completely passive, not to say shined a thousand fires in abstention on the scene, especially since his party was not in power during that time.

But as for Donald Trump, he motivated more than a hundred employees of his construction companies with all kinds of expertise and skills to come to the aid of the CAPITAL OF THE WORLD IN DANGER, NEW YORK CITY. So already, we could deduce that between Donald Trump and Joe Biden, it is day and night. For the first one, he dreams of a prosperous and well-secured United States. As for the latter, it is night opting for a backward United States.

As a result, it wasn't without reason that his late appearance in intervening in favor of Israel was dictated by a considerable loss of 11 percent of votes according to the polls, which pushed his supporters to force him to make this completely circumstantial and in extremis statement in favor of Israel. This is so true, don't you see that aid opted for Ukraine by the tandem Biden-Shumer is more important to them compared to aid for Israel and the security of our borders?

If we correctly understand the game played by this famous duo in question, President Biden would have seemed to force himself to speak in favor of Israel. However, according to other sources, it should be entirely against his own will! Besides, in concert with his conniving right hand, Senator Schumer, don't we see that a question of, "give me first for Ukraine, then I would see if it is possible for Israel and for border security"? So, we have thought to put it in the conditional because of the way this liberal and careless Senator of the great State of New York expressed it.

Also, that leads us to elude the NBC program titled: Deal or No Deal!!. On this particular segment, it should be the job of the media, not precisely that of the power, to inform the American people how this current administration manages to put their interest aside, while taking good care of Ukrainians. The question to ask, since when did this administration propose an increase for the hard-working class, see to give a raise to the Senior Citizens? How long have our poor senior citizens received an increase on their small monthly paycheck?

But yet, Ukraine has been at war for more than two years! It's no longer a secret that Ukraine is a devastated country, as well as deserted and almost a state where it has suffered considerable losses in human life and in infrastructures. Ukraine is not the poorest country in the world, but Ukraine is neither a country where people lead a living quite decently, economically speaking. What we cannot say erotically, given how the angelic beauty of its people is in the spotlight. To the contrary to Hunter Biden, whose salary is multiple times higher than the president of this country, in question, as for you, if you look at a well-paid job, your best bet will never be Ukraine! But despite all that, that doesn't prevent this country from being able to increase the salary of the people by 25.2%?

To have a crystal clear idea of it, the average salary of a regular or hard-working class in Ukraine in 2022 was 399 US dollars a month. In 2023, it passed at 500 dollars (18,529 Hryvnias). What does that mean to you, American people? So, you can see how this administration has become crazy to borrow respectively a billion dollars from China and Japan on a daily basis to please Zelenski and his people, while the

American people, for the most part, beg from day to day to put the meal on their table.

But then, without being too biased, it must be said that there is a little increase in salary, which is really nothing, according to several senior citizens calling to receive it. Are they right to consider it as being nothing that much? Although, the government is delighted to use it as propaganda to show off! As we mentioned above, compared to the Ukrainians one's, which is 25.2%, our senior citizens have just benefited from an increase of 3.2% of their social security check starting on January 1, 2024. Having contacted a senior who's a family member of mine, the latter told me that an increase of 3.2% is almost nothing compared to the exorbitant daily cost of living lately!

So, this is what the traditional media has failed to accomplish by informing and educating people and also letting them know that all these leaders who say they care about Americans are just words of wind that the wind carries and blows before their door. Unfortunately for President Biden, the damage was already done! Whatever happens, this will in no way change the attitude of the voters who already interpreted this gesture as being an opportunistic reaction from Biden similar to a horse that already deserted the farm, while Mr. The President waited until at the last moment ordering to close the gate.

Therefore, in a sense of comparison of both leaders, Trump and Biden, the question that more than one would ask: Does being a real Americanophile mean dishonor and a crime for the country in question? Why didn't all those regrettable incidents occur during Trump leadership? To answer this question of patriotic feeling and love felt for his country, Trump's love and admiration in this regard should serve as a model for everyone to learn to love this country. In this sense, on the contrary to others putting aside this sentiment and character of the nation, they must be conscious of their error to return to the civism which is a sentiment guiding someone how to learn to love and respect his or her country.

In this context, we believe that the world would be a better place to live if people in different countries felt a similar sense of love and patriotism for their native land just as Donald Trump does in regard to the United States! Unfortunately, it is regrettable to see many American people who have always been proud to be Americans, let themselves be carried away by liberal policies of anti-patriots and sellers of the country to push them to prefer corruption and anarchy to discipline and progress.

It is really crucial and alarming to see the number one son of the number one personage of the world, the richest country on earth swimming through those kinds of shenanigans and dirty duties! And what's worse, all this happened not only under his father's beard, Biden, but also under the supervision of the latter who is the commander in chief of the entire nation. Why doesn't the whole world say it often! What a debasement for our dear United States, the country considered as that of our pride and dreams!

Even when it is often said that to everything there is time, we would have never believed that President Biden was going to adopt such a joke and nonsense policy against the country, especially in the area of immigration where former president Bill Clinton, from the same party as him, categorically opposed such migratory disorders. knowing how much is often fatal for a country to let thousands, see currently, many millions of illegal migrants and criminals of all kinds enter its soil. And just like Donald Trump, he did explain his opposition to the American people. And everybody agreed!

Therefore, even when politics is what we call hatred, personal ambition, dirty work, and balance of power, President Biden should in no way allow himself the luxury of doing so. Such a careless attitude is considered wickedness and a great harm done to the country. Even if Biden and Trump are always at loggerheads, when it comes to a good policy adopted for the USA, either President Biden or President Trump has no right to destroy it, for the United States of America must come first before all! We must note that the nation remains, while a president is only elected for 4 years.

Fortunately, Donald Trump is like a fishbone sticking in the throat of any supporter of evil who wants to destroy him as well. This plot has been established since 2015, the same day he announced his candidacy for the presidency of the United States. This plot also hatched against him. Instead of going away despite all the suffering they made him endure, he has currently taken more momentum, especially with some of his ex-collaborators and members of his government having fallen. They fall to the extent of taking advantage of the dictatorial measures taken by Joe Biden against Trump to also storm the void that the latter will have left, perhaps according to their erroneous prediction, his ex-members once convicted. Fortunately, MAGA supporters don't turn a deaf ear and play blindfolded. They are all quickly identified by Trump's supporters, making them unrecognizable and reducing their strength to nothing according to the polls posted everywhere in the fifty states of the country. Meanwhile, Donald Trump remains the only rooster that crows in this barnyard, dragging all of them behind him by an incalculable margin of respectively 40, 56, 60 points, all these former rebel supporters who have now become his fierce opponents. Fortunately for Trump again, they are all already beached on the MAGA reef. This time, the voices of the voiceless open their eyes to send a clear crystal message to the fake leaders, namely: Since 2009, the devils have always pushed us back and this, against our own willingness on the prowl and places led by false politicians who too often, throw us off course. Therefore, it's never too late as human beings to recognize our mistakes and make corrections. All this is to know that American people are waking up from their most profound sleep to largely open their eyes to detect the truth of the false, assuming that the late Biden's statement regarding the dirty red burning between Israel and Palestine has not come from his most profound heart, but of preference because of the gravity of this crisis, putting him in a situation of a dead end through which he does not know what exactly the real trajectory to take to avoid the worst, especially when surrounded by supporters and colleagues with full left ideology and also empty of brains. Of course, as the old adage often said, it's always the tone that makes the music. It has been approved even in the superlative if we can interpret it that way, as much as President Biden's first try through these kinds of presentations. Sometimes, appearance is mistaken, but what looks alike gathers to repeat after the other. Referring to ourselves to such an old adage, is to make an allusion to Jimmy Carter practicing a policy of letting go to plunge the country into bitter tastes just only after two years of bad governance. Therefore, with Biden in power after almost three years, the country is experiencing a similar situation, not to say worse! Despite this tight resemblance, President Jimmy Carter benefited from a certain credibility unlike Biden because he was neither a dictator nor a persecutor, taking advantage of the power as president to hunt down his opponents. Unfortunately, a Banana Republic way is practiced by the President against Donald Trump. Among other things, everyone knows that on July 4th, it is traditional that the barbecue be in the spotlight everywhere in this country because this is a day traducing the historical sentiment of bravery and celebration of joy for the American people. Therefore, October 7th, 2023, testified to the contrary where Israel was under attack. It was not a day of celebration. It was a day where the main ally of the USA was attacked by our notorious enemies! Why not even a single one of Biden's collaborators intervene with a suggestion to reschedule that event, especially when we know that between these two countries, it is like father and son, given this cordial relationship? Don't people always say: All Israel's bad heartbeats correspond to the pulse of the United States? But if that is so, why did this barbecue program continue its long journey in the temporary home (White House) of President Biden? In this sense, through social media, comments continue to hit the mark. Some are more erroneous than others according to the authors, whether they are Republicans or Democrats; Israelis or Palestinians. The questions are these: Is there a personal problem between the Biden Administration and that of Netanyahu? Is there also a question of votes, given that we are approaching a critical election period for Democrats, specifically for President Biden? To these two questions, certain critics tend to make us believe that far from being a matter of votes, it would be preferably a matter of birthright often applied by several families, more precisely between big brother and little brother where either the reason or the guilt of the oldest is always the better. But what a lot of leaders ignore as fact, is that politics doesn't take into account your maturity and experience in this area. When you lead poorly, all experience is of no use and reduced to nothing. Thus, it is in a similar situation that Biden is currently finding himself tortured, not knowing which side of the card to play on not to collapse the country into an abyss. So, to know more about Biden's calvary, one would have to be close to him to recognize that with this question of Israel-Palestine-Ukraine, that means that Biden is having a hard time, to say the least. A severe trip in the leg, preventing him from moving an inch while the polls continue to decline considerably against him. Also, depending on the gravity of this political crisis lately, it seems that Biden and his party are comparable to a car in the middle of a cliff where the road is snowy and slippery and the slightest turn of the wheel is enough for a collapse.

Taking such a path is just to make readers understand that on both sides, it would seem that the evil is infinite for President Biden. On the one hand, he's trying by all means to hide himself behind the curtains so as not to lose the confidence of the 9 million American Jews living in this country. On the other hand, the Palestinian-Americans, who number approximately around 300,000 in the United States, are as angry as a nuclear bomb against Joe Biden. To testify to its veracity, the recent polls in Michigan, being one of the main bastions of the Palestinians after Paterson, New Jersey, it appears that they have already announced the color to liquidate and collapse Biden in 2024. Isn't that what explains that Donald Trump is already up over Biden by 3 points, according to the latest polls? Praise the Lord! Thanks also to technology! It took all of social networks over 40 years to realize a colossal effort to inform and educate people by also allowing them to discover and recognize the true face of our leaders, especially the Democrats'. Praise God once again to have opened our eyes. Because of this clarity, we are actually more mature to widely detect all the fake promises of the Democrats who prefer to give more benefits to illegal immigrants than to us as Americans who are the hardworking class and senior citizens of this country living not even from hand to mouth.

CRISES AND CONTRAST: NAVIGATING THROUGH SOCIO-POLITICAL-ECONOMICAL TURBULENCE

It is no longer a secret that the country is going through a very critical socio-political and economic crisis where also the civism and pride of our emblem, which are our Flag and our national Anthem, are shunned and despised by our own athletes worldwide. All this, added to the problems of all kinds to which we already faced, tend to plunge our fellow Americans further into a system of upside-down life and dead ends.

It's quite crucial for the middle class, especially the hard-working class living in a state of unparalleled. And this, from day one to the actual moment where President Joe Biden stormed the White House through a dodgy and contentious election where Donald Trump's supporters, including himself, shouted out: Penalty! goal scored by hand!

Anyway, if so, it was already too late to rectify the situation since the goal was already validated by the referees of the State of Pennsylvania early on Saturday, November 07, 2020. But it's a pity! However, it remains to know how to correct it to continue to consider us as the strongest of all kinds on this planet as was the case in 1984-1985 with a Ronald Reagan all fire, all flame.

The United States of America is a sacred and a paradise gift from Beyond that no one can snatch from us.

Let's swear that we will never allow anyone to snatch this sacred heritage from us to entrust it either to China or Russia!

To prevent such a well-planned incident orchestrated by the left from happening again. For this particular reason, the only leader of the moment around whom we must regroup is named Donald Trump for a job well-started, but unfinished because of the wickedness of others in 2017-2020. This time is subject to be well accomplished in 2025-2029 for a USA GREAT AGAIN.

However, in contrast to Trump's agenda of ensuring prosperity, security for an adequate immigration system is quite overhauled and corrected where anyone obeying the law in this concern must have free access to visit and stay in this marvelous USA respecting what dictates the law.

A country where freedom of speech always remains the fundamental point for a correct democracy which tends to make our country, contrary to China, Russia flourishing, rejuvenate and mature for an economic system quite stable, equitable and profitable for all Americans. But President Biden on the other side didn't see it with a good eye, deeming it necessary to spend the last two and a half years delivering only failures and crises on the American people where according to a credible source that we can trust, 178 million taxpayers have accused a deficit of 672 dollars a year on their income.

In this optic, a little elementary math is essential to get an idea of it (672×178,000,000 = $119,616,000,000 for his two and a half year in power). Therefore, despite all, it seems Biden is the only one knowing the secret in the matter of managing business to be safe. To have an idea, according to Forbes Financial Journal, during Biden's years as Vice-President until 2017, his net worth was 2.5 million dollars. However, currently speaking, the same said net worth has just taken a cruising speed super and ultra high to fly like an Eagle accusing an exorbitant and spectacular increase of 6.5 million dollars in a lapse of time, President Joe Biden's net worth has passed from 2.5 million to 9 million dollars actually despite this terrible cost of living and inflation that the country has been going through.

In this context, it appears to repeat ourselves, as mentioned above, President Biden is the only one retaining God's secrets to know how to convert the number 2.5 million into 9 million in a record time!

On this point of view, one might refer to elders who used to say: when fools grant advantages to Biden, it was up to the latter, just like them to be stupid not to take the upper hand of them. Of course, it should be a grave problem that President Biden, as a tough Senator in office for almost over forty years and also Vice President to be finally President of this country, having a net worth evaluating at 9 million dollars, should not be a big deal!

But nevertheless, the relevant question to ask: What is the name of the business managed by Joe Biden? How many union members who he always self-proclaimed being leaders hired? Where are these companies located? To all these questions, it's difficult to get a positive answer. For this reason, it's considered cheated and sinful.

Trump on the other side has shown himself to be loyal, conscientious and serious. By the way, let us have an idea of how Trump began to stop the tide of China.

With China's Covid-19 ravaging the world, the barrel of oil had fallen to a derisory price. Trump, who not only had begun to drill in order to make the United States fully independent of gas and oil, was about to purchase several billions of barrels from other countries producing oil at cheap prices, while allowing us to keep our productions quite intact.

You imagine how many trillions of dollars of profits would be realized by buying billions of barrels at 15, 20 dollars in 2020, while reselling at 90 dollars actually to the allied countries? You can also imagine how Trump would have the chance to control and stabilize the price of gas and oil for the full benefit and relief of the American people. It was going to be an amazing and colossal profit for our country. By the way, for your memory and archives, the United States is the largest producer of oil and gas in the world.

That's why Trump had always said: how to beg Saudi Arabia, Venezuela, Iraq for oil when we are the number one producer and have the best quality of oil and gas in the world?

According to statistics well documented, we have a capacity of daily production evaluated at more than 19 million barrels, while Saudi Arabia and Russia respectively are evaluated at 11.81 million and 11 million barrels.

So the question everyone would ask is: why did President Biden, on the very first day in office, stop all of Trump's rentable projects for the country to bring his own political ones, which have since then plunged the country into a geopolitical crisis, not to resurface?

In this sense, Trump represents the daylight for the country, while Biden, the darkness of the night. Also, unlike Biden, Trump did not take advantage of his power as President to hoard and abuse the taxpayers' money.

To the contrary, according to the same financial magazine, Forbes, Trump was better rated and better off financially when he was a simple private business citizen than when he was president. This same source has revealed that in 2017, Donald Trump's net worth showed a balance of 3-5 billion dollars. Therefore, during his presidency, from 2018 to 2021, to end today, 2023, his net worth is estimated at 2.3 billion dollars. An enormous deficit balance of 1-2 billion dollars that Trump never complains about. And that's what makes people appreciate this guy; he never feels any regret! And this is good enough to see that between Trump and Biden, it's day and night for more than 100 million Americans, actually compared to 2020.

For all these reasons, it is imperative that all the fellow Americans avoid the path of the road to Biden to finish K/O Technic this country with another four years in the White House. Further, it seems that Biden is well imbued with the situation in Ukraine. Thus, just the way he conceives American people like wild ducks to mislead them with arrogant lies of all kinds, he has just quite recently repeated it when meeting with his European allies to proclaim victory in

Ukraine. And that, until this time he quoted, if Putin does not cry, it is because he is very audacious and full of cunning. But what I do know, he quoted again, is that Putin is just counting the days to pack up.

That's why interviewed by Tucker Carlson, the retired Colonel American, a very full and well made in this field was quite surprised when he was asked what he thinks of the Russia-Ukraine war that Joe Biden arrogated himself the right to declare widely, victory before his European allies, namely he retains the big wind in his sails to make it difficult for Putin! But, according to this Colonel in question, he found such a statement ultra exaggerated, which has nothing to do with the reality of facts. Without going further Tucker he quoted, how to proclaim victory when you're down 4 to 1 in Ukraine? To be more accurate, he believed that the number of Russians killed in the war is approximately 50 thousand, not including some 40 thousand wounded. While Ukraine has already registered a toll of 200,000 deaths without counting an unimaginable case of casualties. "I don't know if it is on paper," he added, "but the numbers can speak for themselves. Would that happen in the future? What I don't know yet for not having a magic stick in my hands to predict the future."

Therefore, through well-planned and developed statistics explained to Tucker and this, for the full comprehension of his audience, Mr. the retired Colonel has revealed that, given the weakness of our military capacity in this field currently speaking, he doesn't think we are on the good trajectory to prevail these days. In this sense, he would let people know that President Biden, talking that way, just talks downstream, but not upstream because the numbers are there. Nevertheless, to back up and stand his opinion, he told Tucker Carlson, "If the President is already so confident and optimistic, why is he still desperately begging Congress for more aid to help Ukraine? If he loves his people, why not have the courage to tell them the truth? If Ukraine already prevailed over Russia, why does President Biden need more money for the war?" Meanwhile, in a sign of appreciation, many believe that the Colonel is right and crystal correct through these kinds of revealing statistics. By the way, this is said, that's the big difference between Joe Biden and Donald Trump.

That one is an idealist dreamer who always exaggerates by trying to achieve impossible missions, making false statements and promises, while this one, Trump, is a pure realist wanting to concretize things upstream unlike Biden, opting for the opposite. However, no one should be surprised by Biden's attitude because it is a feeling that is quite customary for him. It seems that lies are his major strengths. Maybe without that, he won't be able to perform well. He exaggerates such, that it sometimes causes him to be off topic.

Not too long ago, a town in Hawaii, Maui, was entirely burning down. President Biden, once arrived on the scene, instead of telling people not to be afraid, "This is the United States of America. We will do everything necessary and this, in a short period of time, to allow you to continue to live your normal lives as usual."

Thus, as president of the United States, my government, as soon as possible, will make an overall assessment of all damages suffered for a prompt solution. Therefore, it was the opposite he had done. He compared the terrible burning destroying an entire town to his house in Delaware, which was barely burnt down when a little fire from his kitchen engulfed the house. "During this time, I was on NBC in Washington giving a press conference," he said. "As a result, I had almost lost my wonderful wife Jill, my cat, and my adorable 1967 Corvette."

In addition to that, what about his speech for Labor Day 2023? President Biden said he feels proud and pleased with the great performance he achieved during less than three years in office. An achievement that the previous administration was not accomplished during its four years in power. But what achievement was he bickering about? That of creating 13 million jobs? Wow! Arch-False, people scream! During this time, I went to a friend's house that I have not seen for a long time, with whom I took the opportunity to watch Biden's speech. But one of my friend's sons, upon listening to

Biden talking about creating 13 million jobs, changed the channel to preferably switch to the one broadcasting the US Open to watch a tennis match, even when he's not really a tennis fan.

Therefore, I was pushed to ask his father, "Why did he show himself indifferent? Why did he do this?" His answer was simple. "He's right, my friend!! So, you imagine Biden congratulating himself on having created these 13 million jobs, while there are five of us in the house, only two of us have jobs! But my dear, I have nothing to reproach my son for such a reaction! He is absolutely right because it's about time to say that we're tired of Biden's liars! We have enough!"

However, personally, although I wanted to listen to Biden's *bllsht* as I used to be accustomed to those kinds of fraudulent words from him, I couldn't do otherwise because there are people who don't tolerate this type of nonsense, especially when they are unemployed, while Biden is lying about it! But just the truth is that Biden included in his labor day speech all 9 million employees' people who were unavailable for work during China's Covid-19, while returning to work after being vaccinated. In the end, instead of 13 million jobs, Biden, if he wasn't an arrogant liar as usual of course, would have said, about 4 million jobs created instead of those 9 million because most of which were already there during the era of Donald Trump.

So, this is just to show and prove how we are trapped with a president, Biden, defrocked and derailed in every way! It's unfortunate that the journalist Peter was not rushed to the scene in Hawaii to ask Biden: "Since the classified documents, just like your Corvette that you almost lost were in the garage, were they not also soaked in water by the super firefighters or destroyed by the fire?"

By the way, Joe Biden is the luckiest President the country has ever known. Having said so, is because despite China's Covid-19, where the whole world was in turmoil, not to say upside down, Donald Trump did leave a safe country with a low rate of unemployment, whether 3.5% including a border almost completed for the full success of a reliable environmental system responding to the wishes that a country demands. So, from there we will be able to take charge of the receptions of immigrants who will either have to visit or reside permanently in this said country in question. The brand-new USA inherited by Biden after Trump's era was already on the verge of emerging in every way. It looks like Trump issued a check to Biden, the only thing for the latter to do was to present it to the teller and sign it up while receiving the cash! The simpler, the better! Instead, just like third world country's Leaders, Biden has deemed it necessary to practice what is called: eye for eye, tooth for tooth policy overwhelming the country to position us where we currently are today.

With regard to anti-patriotic behavior, act of corruption of all kinds, including almost total contempt for the supreme God on whom this country has to emblem and symbolize its currency as a sign of belief (IN GOD WE TRUST), one is inclined to ask: where do these changes come from, transforming the belief and the character of American people? Why also, despite forcing, they accept to put aside all the good things done by such a concept? Why not finally having a good memory, making the pride of the country by rendering it respected by all others around the world? Is it like the Bible said, prophecy, already begins.

If so, why should it be right here in the United States that it would have started?

To this question, we can squarely answer in the negative because one has already registered hundreds of thousands of immigrants, not to mention several millions from all over the world who even today are thirsty to come and live in the land of dreams.

So, this opinion tending to make us believe it is a matter of prophecy which is about to be fulfilled, is false. Far from being an Atheist to contradict the bible, one would simply say that this loss of identity and character as the most respected nation on the planet, has come from the weakness of our states and educational institutions filled simply with full heads instead of well-made ones.

Why do Americans let themselves be overwhelmed by the leftists whose ideology is to plunge the country into disarray and total anarchy? How can one explain that he or she follows the trajectory of a simple actress activist populist of the caliber of Whoopi Goldberg whose actions are always ultra-liberal and anarchist. Therefore, she played a good role in a fictional movie which has nothing to do with the reality of facts, and that's all!

But in view of the serious matters and in terms of social projects, such as economy, environment, education to name a few, it's very unwise to take advice from these kinds of professional activists-populists whose essential role is to say nonsense instead of a good topic on big projects for the country where the divergence of ideas between one and the other could bring out the light. That's in this regard I felt ashamed for Senator Ted Cruz when he did accept to sit down with this solid leftist team (NBC), especially the one named above, to discuss nothing and answer impossible and senseless questions! Of course, it is a matter of democracy where we cannot refuse to give an interview to a Radio or TV character.

However, this TV character in question, as the host of the show, lets events overtake her to talk about useless and futile expressions. Through such partisan and disrespectful behavior towards Senator Ted Cruz, the latter would have to backtrack and turn back to say openly to Whoopi Goldberg: "I regret saying it to you, Whoopi. However, it will be quite ugly to reach a mutual understanding since we did not attend the same political school. Without wanting to have an elite attitude to be arrogant, I'm above all a lawmaker always opting for the principles of the law to be the compass of the United States, which has nothing to envy with comedy and nonsense. But on the other hand, before having accepted your invitation to come to the show, I had to know that since we didn't attend the same political institution, it was going to be very difficult to be on the same pedestal for common ground. So if that is so, to repeat after the other: each Donkey must bray in his own pasture!" By the way, that incident already occurred; let's forget about it hoping that Ted Cruz, next time will avoid such a waste of time with people without faith nor the law of this window.

Among other things, for the United States to remain solid and keep quite intact its laurels conquered on the battlefield, the country must avoid losing its historical memories, which are one of the avant-garde factors which always lead to a good trajectory because a country which is deprived of them, is a country without a great and memorable future. However, when we retain a good memory to figure out and know how huge these laurels are, we must act so that they stay and remain intact of which nothing will disturb the limpidity and clarity.

Referring to all of this, is to let us know that there was a time where Americans were the most respected people on earth, especially in matters of generosity regarding other people in need. I remember having observed with my own eyes Guide Tour Chauffeurs who were fighting each other for dealing with American Tourists rather than other nations, such as French for instance, although they were more comfortable speaking French than English. Why such a preference and appreciation for American Clients?

The answer was: "Americans are generous and courteous by not only saying thank you very much, but also make you happy by a good gratification for rendered services." Asking them also the Guide Chauffeurs, what about Canadian Tourists and others? "There is no comparison. American Tourists at first, I'm telling you!" But during this last time, that has just started changing where this sign of appreciation has suffered a considerable decrease. It was not that long that surprisingly I met a gentleman in a club in New York City coming from the Czech Republic.

I did ask him if he decides to stay here permanently. He was not quite pleased with my question telling me: "I'm a technician in my country. I'm well secured, too! There's no reason for me to switch for the USA, especially when I have learned how even the middle-class over here is struggling actually." Thus, referring to different news media that used to support the dead-end Biden's policy, it would seem, they too, have started being conscientious of the reality of facts. If I can parody CNN (5-26 and 09-06-2023), it is revealed that two-thirds of the democrats have disapproved of Biden's policy and his option to wear the uniform of the party in the 2024 election. If it is majoritarily accurate, it should not be a small taste! It should be a serious wound that the party in power suffers and this from the very breakthrough of the Biden at the head of the first magistracy of the country.

Unfortunately, all is not yet crystal clear. Perhaps everything seems just a rumor circulating around Washington by the supporters of the ruling team either to confuse their Republican opponents or induce them in error as usual. Meanwhile, it is revealed that Biden is up by 2 points over Donald Trump.

Despite there never being smoke without fire, the media, as usual, interfere to blur and bias the map. Anyway, it is often said again there's never smoke without fire. If so, will they call Michelle Obama or Hillary Clinton to take over? No one can yet arrogate the right to say that a lot of speculation has already been revealed.

The former protégé and Obama's right hand, not to mention her boss as it will be described further, seemed to applaud those rumors, especially when she was quite pleased to answer these sweet deal questions from her favorite host icon Rachel of MSNBC when she learned that Trump would be going to jail in GA. Unfortunately, if Rachel was flattered to have her idol leader on the show, therefore the audience was not convinced. Just to say that Hillary didn't reap good fruits. What demands that Hillary return home to finally admit that everything is over. All that remains is ashes! Hillary must know that despite her being the real Hillary, all fire, all flame then, she has been taken in a sandwich by Donald Trump in 2017, why did she think she could emerge again? By the way, some two weeks after, she was forced to resurface Russia - because the phase of the things that have just changed would have proved the contrary in the matter of the Georgia electoral scandal. As a result, Donald Trump had raised an exorbitant amount of 10 million dollars in only one day! What was going to happen within two weeks after that the left oligarch media would not turn any more deaf ear recognizing the great weakness of Joe Biden in the function.

For this particular reason, seeing that Trump has become very popular over Biden leading him by over 10 points, Hillary has started again to sing the same song, namely 'another interference Russia 2024, watch out! What Hillary would try to do, is to become specific to the roaches which can't eat the food, but they make sure they spoil it. However, according to more than one, Hillary has just proven once again that she's a real moron in matters of politics, not to say, dwarf! because without knowing perhaps, she gave a big favor to Donald Trump's supporters, that of allowing them to know that the leader of the MAGA is already the winner of the rendez-vous election of November 5, 2024 because history is an eternal start over again! That is exactly the same tactic she used to blow people's minds in 2017. By the way, one of her right hand, Donna Brazile, who tried to cheat with her during the first presidential debate in 2017 VS. TRUMP, would make it clear before Hillary that Trump's movement is not a small task!

Things as a veteran in this field she had never seen before! But the latter preferred to turn a deaf ear and play blindfold instead to admit for true that it is quite phenomenal and unbeatable.

What about Michelle Obama considered as the front winner of the Democratic party? We don't know if it was a so-called popularity of the old date. But time has passed and many scandals that are stored up during their reign are breaking the ceiling and that also many cats are about to be out of the bag to resurface again.

From this, will the voters turn a deaf ear and remain blindfolded as it was the case in 2007 and 2020? How do you expect Michelle Obama is going to do better? Without wanting to go through other details, was it not under Barack Obama's leadership that Joe Biden realized all the shenanigans with Russia, China, Romania, and Ukraine?

Therefore, it appears that on both sides the evil will be infinite for the Democrats in 2024. Thus, this injury in question, before it has proved to be an incurable cancer, requires urgent care from Dr. Donald Trump in 2024.

Without doubt, although facing criminal justice, he's the only one actually who has the wind in his sails capable of turning the tide and being able to remedy it. Nevertheless, another four more years with the tandem Biden-Kamala will be sadder for our wonderful USA. But what we must know is that only in a dictatorial country, it is admitted that the recognition of well done is cowardly.

For us Americans, as a civilized country respecting Republican standards, we will always go back to the past to evaluate and recognize the good deeds of a leader. We cannot allow ourselves to be carried away by fanaticism which is always a feeling contrary not only to reason, but also to the smooth running of a country. It is in this sense that we henceforth tell everyone to swear to vote: patriotism, economy and military security, good pay work, progress, and education while rejecting anarchy, incompetence, partisanship, and electoral shenanigans. Also, now is the time for all loyal patriots through this current crisis this country is going through to proudly showcase their sincere love for this AMAZING nation by redeeming it from the clutches of Biden and his cronies in Washington DC.

In this optic, we with one voice, we recommend our dear consistent and loyal compatriots to understand that these are challenges that we had already taken up! And this, on several occasions when the country was in danger.

Without going any further, don't we remember when the ultra-liberal farmer, in reference to Jimmy Carter, 1977-1981, a true Joe Biden, was on the point to collapse the country by his famous policy of letting go of corruptions of all kinds, you fervent compatriots, you did not realize your belonging to politics. You said out loud: no to politics in

Carterian jumble. You chose magnanimously Ronald Reagan to take over on January 20, 1981 while once swearing in and correcting all the misdeeds bequeathed to us by the famous pastor-farmer from Georgia as a legacy of bad experiences.

All of this is to say that these kinds of liberal, partisan, and corrupt policies always lead a country into the abyss to no resurface. However, if your memory does not fail you, you must have the courage to not only appreciate but also admit for real that with the breakthrough of RONALD REAGAN in power, in concert with the Republicans including Democrats by principle, he managed to put all his international adversaries K/O technique to make USA the true number one, from North to South, and East to West of the planet.

If history is really the truthful account of past events, how can we forget such a good deed?

These three times, past, present, and future, are always in perfect connection to each other because it is from 1981-1989, 2017-2021 respectively, to properly evaluate and analyze Jimmy Carter of 1977 and Joe Biden, actually speaking, to make a judicious choice in 2024, avoiding again prioritizing anarchy, incompetence, corruptions over honesty, competence, and patriotism.

In this sense, it is important to remember that a people without good memory is a people without a promising future.

One needs to do long research to know what to do before fulfilling your civic duty during election day. As American Citizens, first think about the actual situation of the USA. Is it in good shape? If not, as voters, when you decide to head to the polls to vote and elect the next President of the United States of America, be ready to make a conscientious examination by asking yourself if life has improved for you since Biden took office. Has your savings account either grown or considerably diminished? Do your children have better opportunities than you did? Is your neighborhood safer, actually?

Joe Biden's reelection depends on his record. Is 38%

approval from his own party a decent record? If not, will you give him a free pass for four more years of disaster? Being a Nation of good historical memory, make sure, as a referee during the "D" day in 2024, you'll carry with you your red card to expel Biden from the White House by returning him to Delaware as you did in 1980 against Jimmy Carter not only for incompetence but also for a well-planned malice and harm caused to the country and the American people.

I remember having seen a young adult gentleman serve 5 years behind bars for having a verbal conversation named Russia and China. Only such a simple mention in that puppet and dependent country, of course, made him endure a sentence of 5 years in jail.

Naturally, Biden is the commander-in-chief of the United States.

However, it is not up to Biden to assume all the mismanagements that the United States has experienced in recent times, especially since one knows that a president who is elected to serve has his ministerial cabinet, his own advisers including senators and party congressmen around him for good governance.

All these people must be considered as the main Joe Biden's collaborators, except if these collaborators and advisors in question are competent, serious, and fervent patriots.

They must be able to sit down with their octogenarian President to tell him that such and such a thing cannot be done like this. They must have the courage and strength by coming out of their graveyard silence to tell Mr. President that negotiating and undertaking contracts in secret with companies of our notorious enemies like China is not a good option for the progress and the safeguard of the United States of America.

But, if like President Biden, his collaborators have deemed necessary to celebrate with open arms his irresponsible and unpatriotic acts, they are more guilty of lack of good governance than Joe Biden himself.

If in 2018, I had a little bit of lack of knowledge about what was going on in the USA under the leadership of

Donald Trump, actually, the whole proof is crystal clear in everyone's eyes to see, verify, and certify that the politics of dogs eating cats practiced by the left came true for the great profit of China through non-existent mafia and voodoo contracts.

Are they not, actually speaking, facing the reality of the facts? When we observe how millions and millions have often maliciously been negotiated and released in the greatest secrets of the Gods, not only for the greater good interest of our tough adversary, which is China, but also for the full and entire satisfaction of the latter whose only objective in mind is that of surpassing and dethroning the United States of America of the worldwide title as being too long the number one in all.

It's not entirely difficult to understand the reason for a whole series of acerb and violent criticism from the left against Donald Trump when he openly accused China of being at the root of the spread of Covid-19 in the world or more precisely here in the United States.

Instead of supporting efforts and strategies used by Trump to protect the interest of the country and limit damages by a whole avalanche of cases already discovered via China, Trump without a blow decided to cut off contact with the opponent until further notice.

As a result, we have been surprised to observe Biden and his partisans firing red bullets at Donald Trump, accusing him of being the greatest troublemaker that the country has ever known in its existence. At that time, all those detaining an idea in terms of political shenanigans already admitted that something was fishy between China and Biden.

It is very unfortunate for this country; this mafioso plot was successful while Donald Trump was the main victim in wanting to defend the country he adores and cherishes so much. On this point of view, one asks the question: is loving his country and his people wholeheartedly a crime or a betrayal?

How many Americans are willing to live their life like Chinese ones, where freedom of speech, protest, and so many other democratic achievements are prohibited? Who among you prefers hell to heaven? If your preference is the last option, swear before the nation that never, you will allow that to happen again! How can one explain that elections have been held since November while until now, one was still in court to prove that the Arizona election was full of scraps claimed by Kari Lake, where the result was still contested by the latter?

Anyway, it is always important to claim your rights because even when the forfeit claimed by Kari Lake would not manage to change the phase of the Arizona electoral game, but at least it would spring the light, allowing voters to have an idea of the way in which leaders have often proceeded to manipulate the electoral system in order to display and give the results of their choice. In other words, as painted artists who decorate the house, they reserve the right to paint it any way they want while giving you the color that suits them. Thus, the insistence and perseverance of the former journalist and candidate for governor, Kari Lake, has already enabled her to carve out a place for herself towards a new horizon, namely that of running for one of the senate seats for her state, Arizona, in 2024.

In this context, given all this electoral hustle and bustle that Arizona has just recently experienced with Kari Lake, nicknamed: the coqueluche and the star of the day and the candidate to defeat, we will take all the necessary measures to ensure that everything will be done in order and discipline so that the infernal and electoral caravan of Kari Lake galloping at full speed to Capitol Hill in order to help her fellow future Republican colleagues to keep on bringing order to the mess of Washington D.C.

Also, do we like to go back, more precisely during the pandemic, to say that Kari Lake, as a journalist, was right when she pointed out that the media was bad for firing too many red balls at Trump. Also, as an ex-journalist, but of course independent unlike Lesley Stahl of 60 minutes, I wonder if she is not thinking to feel guilty while having a share of responsibility for the current crisis that the U.S. is going through?

If I were Trump's adviser, I would have told him not to accept such an invitation. But there again, it would not be advantageous to him, especially since we were at a dangerous crossroads not only with the pandemic, defunding the police fund, and so many others.

The way this Journalist went about plucking, devastating, and debating Trump, means he's the worst pet peeve that the U.S. has ever known before. She even managed to say that Trump would be at the roots of the celestial anger, that is to say: GOD DOESN'T LIKE YOU, MR. THE PRESIDENT!

However, what she didn't remember is that Trump was the very first to accuse China as being the main culprit and that emergency measures must be taken to prevent any flight from China from landing on our tracks until everything is clear. She knew it very well! However, to smear Donald Trump's image, professional of trade that she is, Mrs. the journalist in question used razor blade sharp language to tell American people, "Look closely at the image of the man you voted for 3 years ago." It was without reason she did ask President Trump: "Why do you want to seek a second term?" Besides, it's always the tone that makes the song! There is no getting out of there. First of all, to start the interview, she said: "Mr. President, I'm going to ask you tough questions. Are you prepared and ready?"

Using such an impulsive interrogation to start an interview with the President of the United States, the first Character of the planet, means pure and simply that Lesley already announced the color to cause the interview to end in a fish tail. Even out of decency for the profession and even respect, but such a bitter taste at first on board, is completely smearing the professional ethic of the profession which always demands: transparency and impartiality. Lesley must have known even in literature, we always begin with weakest quotes including politics!

So more than one would ask the question: how does she

feel now when she painted Donald Trump of all the wrong colors in the world? Is the US better and safer than 3 years ago? If not, a mea culpa is quite necessary not to say sine qua non from this journalist in question imploring pardon for having badly criticized and induced American voters in error.

Yes, if she really loves her job as a journalist, including the country and its people, she must have the courage to confess to herself the sin and harm done to people who went to the polls to fulfill their civic duty and give their voice in this electoral process of 2020.

These kinds of professional journalists who are true experts in matters of the caliber of the one mentioned above, know full well that in politics, it's always nice talk that gets voters going and that happened on November 4, 2020.

They managed to pass the milestone, but the fact remains that it was not a magnanimous victory as was the case in 2017 where Donald Trump had provoked the real panic in the camps of the democrats by making them vocifer and groan bitterly all the fanatics of Hillary Clinton including superstars like Madonna, Jay Z-Beyonce, Bonjovi, Lebron James, Lady Gaga to only name a few by a victory in apotheosis. Compared to 2017 victory over the weakest candidate of the democratic party after Walter Mondale, we are all agree and considered Biden's victory as the one called in the 17th century: "DEFEAT AN OPPONENT WITHOUT PERIL, SIMPLY MEANS A TRIUMPH WITH NO HONOR AND GLORY."

In this context, it should be always better to lose with pride and honor than to win with force and dishonesty parodying leaders of third world countries when they usually say: "Power is not given, power is taken."

Winning that way means also force taking precedence over right what is always of short time of power. It's not without reason that Biden's so-called revolution is now eating its own supporters and sons. Real observers in the matters consider it as a hypothetical and threatened power that was not built on a privileged system to stay and be sustained.

In the contrary, the GOP in its MAGA slogan, as the loser of 2020 is about to quickly take flight like an eagle to leap higher than everyone else on the little White Horse located in 1600 Pennsylvania Avenue, Washington DC. to clean up Biden's mess and reach the pinnacle for the good of the United States by making it GREAT AGAIN.

NAVIGATING THE COMPLEX LANDSCAPE OF POLITICAL FORGIVENESS AND INTEGRITY

Many say that Trump is not a politician because in politics we don't forgive. Among his supporters and partisans are angry that Trump failed to take advantage of Biden's mental weakness including so many others whom we refrain from listening to fire red balls at the latter.

On this point, it should be noted that the one who claims to forgive others who have wronged you, has made no restriction to this word. This expression of, in politics, we do not forgive, comes from the world, outside of this world, forgiveness is heavenly.

Moreover, President Biden is an American. If Trump always says, "America first," it will be irrelevant to criticize Biden's state of health and mentality afterwards. Trump might feel frustrated for leaving a country in good trajectory of progress for Biden while the latter along with his political acolytes would like to transform it into a defrocked Venezuela or Haiti. So he may hate what Biden has done as bad for the country, not Biden personally as an American.

It's not without reason, answering to the questions of several journalists such as Sean Hannity and others, he has always tried to not insist too much on three recent occasions where Biden has just collapsed in full middle of the marine academic graduation session, followed by the forgetting of the navy's name to whom he wanted to honor for his good accomplishment, finally culminating in his recent visit to Ireland where he flatly forgot the name of the country while recently staying there for three days. By the way, Trump was forced lately to joke about Biden's health. But it was not from his heart. As politics is a matter of balance of power, he was forced to do so to create an atmosphere of humor for the delectation of his fans.

As the Greek expression says: "from your lips to God's ear" hoping that the bad is already done that American voters realize all those in their power and their comprehension to avoid a repeat of a democrat leader of Biden's caliber.

In this context, one says that age always brings reason. However, what we see is that Biden is an exception to this rule while making preposterous decisions that only lead us into the abyss! What we call an old man who is messy, disoriented, and disorganized. Therefore, far from being predestined and also someone having a magic wand to predict the future, what we know is that we're all placed under the banner of the universe, which often acts by showing signs that will tell how your day is actually and how tomorrow will be. But it seems that Americans for the most part don't pay attention to it.

All of this is to say that no one needs to be panicked about Joe Biden's ability to get back on this little white horse of Washington DC's Pennsylvania Avenue in 2024, not only for reasons mentioned before, but also for those that will follow.

First of all, during the presidency of Joe Biden, compared to 1998 when statistics revealed that 62% of Americans had faith in our institutions, justice, religions, education, and others, this figure has gone considerably decreasing in recent times to drop squarely to only 32% of Americans who trust the State. Nevertheless, such a decline is really scary, jeopardizing a promising future of our wonderful US, especially prosecuting your main opponent, such as Donald Trump, instead of proving to 65 percent of your own party, whose opinion revealed you didn't quite win, catholically speaking. And what about the Republicans who 90 percent still believe the 2020 elections were rigged?

Either way, all hope is not lost. There is still a way for this country to regain confidence as long as the media realizes the seriousness of the situation and is prepared to openly talk about it to the American people instead of turning a deaf ear and hiding it, this declined statistic as it did for Joe Biden during the 2020 election period.

It makes us sad to see that lawyers such as Senator Charles Schumer and Congressman Johnson, two outstanding democrats in the Biden administration, are unaware that American people are brain-dealing people to take the risk of saying that everyone sees we have a fertility problem in the country.

In this context, we must fill the void with immigrants to whom we must give free access to reside and become American Citizens. As far as the other, that of Congressman Johnson who added: To prevent immigrants from entering this country is purely to prevent American people from having food on their plate.

What seems funny in the declaration of Charles Schumer is that a man of law also bears the same first name as the great French philosopher of the 18th century, Montesquieu, the main founder of the principle of natural law and separation of the three powers. You want to tell me the famous liberal senator did not know how to have the decency to follow the same trajectory as the latter for a strict and adequate application of the law? Thus, from the Godfather of the law in question, if we nickname him that way, Charles Montesquieu, "useless law always weakens the necessary law." For the good memory of the two so-called men of law in the Biden administration, that means when the law ceases to be executed as it should, only from corruptions of the republic, the state is already lost. Didn't these liberal men of law know that?

However, Trump, who is not a lawyer, unlike Biden, the

latter who had been wading through it for nearly half a century, quickly understood for a country to move forward towards progress, Montesquieu's doctrine must always be implemented and practiced in its entirety with the separation of the three powers independently from each other so that none of them be above the law. This is in this sense that, far from being racist in this regard, Donald Trump always refers himself to the principles of the great French philosopher for a reliable immigration whose respect for the law will always be at the forefront. Thus, going the right way will show the mutual respect between the immigrants and the United States for progress and peace.

Donald Trump's philosophy as a fervent student of the principles of good sitting leads him to believe that when everything is in order and discipline, we will see a USA very happy, prosperous, and GREAT AGAIN as it takes its flight like an eagle towards its destiny which is the Climax.

Therefore, if in France, Germany, England, and even in the Dominican Republic, to name a few, there are laws that establish how to regularize the status of the people to know when and how, the duration of their stay, their accommodation, and others, why not the United States, too?

Let's stop talking about racism and discrimination which are useless. On the contrary, let's talk about law, discipline, duration of the immigrants' stay, their accommodation, and mutual respect for each other. Doing so will make us a civilized nation welcoming everyone without prejudice of race and color instead of discrediting each other with futile and trivial expressions.

Let's go back to the thoughtless and erroneous statement issued by Senator Charles Schumer about fertility problems and filling the void with immigrants. We highly doubt there is such a shortage on the American side. And if there is, the left and right policy formulated by liberals of the caliber of Schumer and his colleagues democrats is the main cause! For example, young adult women have the right to undergo any kind of transformation in any gender, including marrying each other. Also, young gentlemen are stuck in the same new system of life. So if this is already or about to happen, it is the big fault of most of the lawmakers who for personal reasons or political ambition have often taken advantage of their majority either in the congress and the senate to vote no matter how, and this outside the norms already established.

What about the justice system? During this last time, we are inclined to observe that contrary to Charles Montesquieu opting for the separation of power between these three concerned instances for the balance and equilibration of the three powers, this is the opposite which has been proved in everyone's eyes where this balance is upside down whether one is democrat or republican in majority respectively in the chamber and the senate.

The role of the judiciary power is to make sure that the law is applied and respected. Lamentably, the contrary has registered, what does not date today and yesterday. Therefore, since 2014 under Obama's leadership, it is a question of blindfold and deaf ear on Russia with his famous Secretary of States who as such, had plenty right to act as she wished while her boss, Barack Obama, practiced the policy of tolerance, by letting the wound worsen because liberal democrats often say: the dirty linens must be washed in families to allow this moribund system to make its merry way. What a shame on Obama!

When we remember how the latter was the object of a flagrant humiliation by Hillary during a debate on one of the liberal TV media where she had to answer a question formulating on the experience and qualification of Obama and John McCain, namely which one of the two being better qualified to be President of the United States?

We were quite surprised by Hillary's response to such a question, namely: Obama did not meet any conditions that could allow him to run for the country's presidential chair. He's only a dwarf in terms of political experience to be the head of this country as the first commandant in chief. As for McCain, as a former war prisoner wearing his senate color for a very long period of time, he is super qualified to ride and gallop the little white horse of Pennsylvania Avenue

Washington DC. That was a response that angered a lot of Black African-Americans who harshly criticized Hillary for betraying the cause of her own party.

These people had advanced as supporting arguments that they could understand that politics is a balance of power where one must always consider oneself at the highest level than one's opponent. But the problem is that John McCain was not a presidential candidate for the Democrat party! This comparison of experience and qualification did not put Obama and Hillary Clinton against each other, but McCain and Obama!

So we think that was the biggest campaign mistake made by this eternal candidate for which African-Americans made her pay the very expensive price by voting by millions, the so-called inexperienced outsider young fresh senator from Chicago, Illinois, to repeat the great regret memory, Rush Limbaugh: Barack Hussein Obama!

By the way, the same people were happy to see Obama not behaving like a resentful President, putting aside all Hillary's diatribes against him and giving her a quite masterful post in his government, that of the Secretary of State for foreign affairs, making Hillary the third most influential person in the world. This was not quite pleasing to the Radical Left, Reverend Farrakhan, when he said in a press conference that Obama was sitting in the car but not really the main driver of the car. Perhaps, without doubt, this would have meant that Obama was a puppet of the system for having been forced to make choices. If so, the current situation of so many shenanigans and irregularities discovered while Biden was Obama's Vice President, including the belligerent behaviors of Hillary Clinton as Foreign Affairs Secretary to retain full power to act as she pleased, thus, without obeying and bending to the commands of hierarchical superiority, could testify to the authenticity and veracity of this. Therefore, we would have believed that Donald Trump had followed the same trajectory as Obama to not provoke and prosecute Hillary, contrary to what he said during the great debate between these two. But still, no one expected that Obama was going to empower Hillary, allowing her to do and undo.

Starting from HAITI, where she gave us a drug dealer and put a prostitute in power. What about LIBYA, where she acted erroneously, where the political situation over there turned into a fishtail, without forgetting a question of China. China's file. A real political scheming to allow her to go it alone. But what we cannot understand is that all that hustle and bustle of politics orchestrated by the so-called the third greatest character of the world was done at Obama's beard, as what would one say that Hillary was the main Commandant in chief while Barack was on the other side as the radical left leader Farrakhan would have well described so!

In this context, it is from the lack of emancipation and separation of power that the state of a country begins to show weakness, to finally be lost. Indisputable proofs have often shown it well.

Fortunately, technology is in a good position to detect and publicize the mismanagement of corrupt leaders even when it is late. From there, people have come out of their ignorance and silence to no longer be seen as wild ducks as we are observing actually. It's not without reason that Trump always says that it's better to lose with dignity and honesty than winning without peril, to triumph without glory.

One that note, you may be asking: why should we choose to vote for DONALD TRUMP IN 2024?

The answer to this question is easy to respond to.

Donald Trump was not a politician. You can observe that it is one of the reasons why he's been victimized since 2016 and this, until the present time. As being a businessman and a frank patriot, he didn't like the way that politicians and traditional corruptors managed to allow other countries to manipulate and take advantage over hard American workers.

The unnecessary war in Iraq was one of the causes pushing Trump to get involved in politics to teach a lesson to the big gray-bearded politicians of the country.

Moreover, it was his biggest challenge during his four years in power. It is not without reason, from his spectacular breakthrough and his entry into the White House, he said, "Something has to change. Our country does not deserve to be used as the wooden horse of other countries exploiting our force, our resources, and our experience to finally conceive us as the stupidest and wild ducks as already mentioned above."

Referring himself to beyond, he refrained after Abraham to continue: "ENOUGH IS ENOUGH! UNITED STATES FIRST!"

A slogan that created so much panic in several sectors of the countries, especially those whose personal interest has been threatened, that is to say, the big gray-bearded politicians without omitting the international countries such as China and Russia, to only name them, our main enemies with only one objective in mind, that of collapsing the United States for being for too long the number one on earth.

INTERIOR AND EXTERIOR PLOT VS. DONALD TRUMP

As an American citizen aware of what the country has done for him, he only needed to be someone ungrateful not to remember all these good things. On this point, only anti-nationalists and anti-patriots who behave selfishly so as not to work for the country continue to produce more BUILDERS of the caliber of Donald Trump. As for national enemies, they are very numerous and belong to the high hierarchy of official authority of the country. And what is worse, the majority of them are in the same political affiliation as Donald Trump. And that is there again, this latter is the most trapped because when your own party criticizes you for the full benefit of others on the other side, you have become what is well named: ALONE VERSUS ALL. And that's what the liberal leftist media had to use to bludgeon Trump to make him look like the main pet peeve of the country. It is not without reason that Donald Trump's name is the easiest to pronounce in the American media, whether more than a million times a day according to statistics that would be credible.

To have an idea of the national coalition against this charismatic leader reformist, Donald Trump, we can name among them Hillary Clinton, who is an everlasting opponent of his, Joe Biden, Nancy Pelosi, Adams, Colin Powell,

George W. Bush, Mitt Romney, Chris Christie, to name a few. Although 75 million people support Trump's revolution, it's not quite enough to make the right recipe since the real strength is not necessarily the quantity, but quality with people who hold the key to power and are part of the high hierarchy. They are the ones who have the power to buy the spoken, written, and televised media at auction. They are the ones who have the say.

It's not without reason the great French writer, La Fontaine, said: The reason for being the strongest is always the best. According to Trump's philosophy, to realize this dream, that is to say, make America great again, we have to move away from these big donors because when they invest 10,000, they claim 1,000,000 in return. In this sense, accepting such a compromise will not make the country AMERICA GREAT AGAIN.

However, what we see is that they try to do everything to block Trump's way. But what they ignore is the existence of fate. They no longer take into account that we are nothing on this earth if not, little things placed and guided by the Universe which orders and governs. Thus, it was no wonder Chris Christie was scared to death like a trapped mouse when he was tested positive during the pandemic fomented by China. By the way, even BIG CHRIS still remains an enraged anti-Trump, given his poor popularity, people don't pay attention to his futilities. This is said, he's been conceived by voters as someone complaining for not being hired by Trump.

However, as far as Republican schemers and treaties, there are numerous on this field. Therefore, the two biggest chameleons among whom further aggravate the convictional situation of Donald Trump for their personal ambition are named: Governor Ronald Dion DeSantis and Nikki Haley. They were considered two right wings of Donald Trump. So these two trusted colleagues of the latter have committed such a blatant betrayal of siding against Trump! Why not take advantage of the situation to beat him up with his own ex-collaborators?

But the question remains: how to proceed to succeed? But it is crystal clear! That of insisting, persisting, and throwing all the energy that it requires to paint Donald Trump in all the rainbow colors of the world to show and prove to American voters that he is the black beast for this country.

That would have been the strategy of Biden and all his subordinates in the justice department to make Donald Trump unpopular, unelectable, hateful, bankrupt, and obsolete before the electoral contest of November 5, 2024. But once again, it was well thought out, but poorly successful, especially since Biden, proceeding in this way, has rendered the biggest favor to Donald Trump, making his popularity grow considerably forever, this throughout the fifty states of the United States.

As far as Biden, a little climate change recently in provenance from Canada, having a little bit of environmental repercussions over certain areas of the US, the latter was already panicking to say: I called Prime Minister Trudeau to find out how to help with army force.

Despite his long period at the helm of environments of nature, Biden fails to understand that you can't prevent Mother Nature from acting when she decides to do her merry way! It is in this sense that we say if these tenacious politicians without faith and law continue to insist on prosecuting Trump to thwart fate, they will pay a dear price.

Far from being afraid, Donald Trump is going to become a stunt for his destroyers. In 2020, more than seventy-five million people supported Trump. However, in 2024, the number will grow as it takes flight like an eagle towards its destiny! What's so difficult to understand? In 2019, it was mostly Republicans who responded to the call of the great gathering.

Today, it is already a whole mixture of political entities which have become aware of the gravity of the situation in the country to ask for mercy to Joe Biden because they think they have a large share of responsibility in this outcry.

In this sense, history will continue for good to make its

way insofar as it is for the first time a former President of the UNITED STATES, currently very far at the head of the poll compared to his opponent Republicans including the incumbent, the actual President himself must come to be indicted!

All who have eyes to look, observe! All who have ears, listen because a wonderful and miraculous event will happen for the first time in the history of the United States. A former President, now a candidate, is being indicted while winning the presidential election by an overwhelming majority of votes and states in 2024. What will be the real reality in all of this? A demon racist and liberal extremist illegitimate regime will end to make way for that of a Republican who will do everything within his reach to advance the country step by step towards the well-being of progress, to make forget the liberal Democrats on the political scene for having caused a lot of damage to the American people. And this, by a lot of scheming, letting go, and incompetence in everything.

After this magnanimous victory in 2024, many supporters and fanatics would expect and think of a revenge policy from Donald Trump against his detractors. Oh no! Not at all! On the contrary, according to what we would perceive in this great book, it will be total forgiveness for all who did contribute to destroy him in flesh, in bone, and in spirit to prevent him from MAGA.

Don't take into consideration what he said during his electoral campaigns. Trump is not a master of himself. He's already born again. The invisible Guy from whom he has received his guidance will never never allow him to act that way. If the same guy always preaches forgiveness, how can we expect a politics of vengeance from Donald Trump on January 20, 2025? Remember that it is always said: what comes out from our mouth does not precisely come out from the heart, which has its own reason the mouth might not understand.

Just like Jesus Christ, Trump will be humble and wise to say: please forgive them all because they didn't know how much he loves his country so much. Trump will have nothing to lose, but everything to gain. We are not going to follow the bad example of Biden's dirty behavior and other countries which often fail by practicing the policy of an eye for an eye and a tooth for a tooth. We must know that acting that way always delays a country towards the path of progress. We are not going there. We, Trumpets, are too smart for that. We are all Americans. Our country first!

How to erase them on the political scene and make them forget if we throw ourselves into the same policy of letting go as them? Trump already knows that we cannot progress if protests and hates have become a pandemic in our country. The goal is to offer good pay jobs to our people so that they live a decent life where stress will not be able to incite them to violence. This is what Donald Trump will carry in his agenda for a USA currently in peril. Furthermore, our objective is crystal clear in front of the American people, that of making forget all destructor Democrats and sellers of this country.

However, to achieve this objective, which is so important for a country already mortgaged and devastated by the Biden administration, we must provide the United States with good governance where principle and law serve as our compass. Thus, with economic stability, peace in the bellies of all Americans where the majority of them are not even living from hand to mouth; absolute security and careful education for our future generation of the country, we believe that Trump will be capable of leaving an unforgettable memory of how to do things well and that each time the left would tend to destroy it as is the case with President Biden, the American people will stand up to say no, giving the red card and putting them out of business to ensure the smooth running of the country that they admire and cherish so much. So, for this particular reason, no matter what is said, there will not be tactics of vengeance under Trump's administration in 2025 compared to Biden's demagogy and BullS**T. Acting that way would be to take the country out of the Hudson River and throw it into the Pacific Ocean.

At the age of seventy-eight years old in 2025, Donald Trump's main goal is to offer to you all a United States of

America Great Again contrary to the recent opinion issued by the weakest and the unpopular ex-Governor of New Jersey with the only 1% of the votes, namely: Bringing Trump back to power is putting all his opponents in danger. What we must learn from such erroneous critics is that a dictator always thinks that other leaders are also dictators like him. Because under his leadership in New Jersey, he tried to destroy one of the Mayors who did not agree with him, he believes in his mind that Trump, once elected in 2024, will follow his same dictatorial example he traced against the Mayor of Fort Lee, New Jersey. Fortunately for him, while sad for his subordinates, it is the innocent who have paid for the guilt. In this context, La Fontaine, one of the greatest of his century would have said: According to whether you will be Mr. CC or his subordinates, the justice in the State of New Jersey finds you innocent or guilty.

For your good comprehension and memory, my friend, Trump will never follow your worst path, which has reduced you to nothing on the political and social spectrum. Don't think that Trump was really blamed by his supporters for having tolerated you watching all his moves in the White House? Perhaps he thought that you were a human being! Look at the way you try to destroy him. Thank God he didn't give you the job that you wanted! Oh, no my friend! It's not at all Trump's priority in 2025 that of hunting witches. Dr. Trump won't have time for nonsense like this. On the contrary, Mister Chris, economy, inflation, good pay jobs, energy, security, borders, our borders, and education, these are the main priorities for MAGA in 2025.

It's not without reason he recently pointed out to all his fellow Americans, I quote: "TODAY, I'M ACCUSED OF ALL THE BAD OMENS THAT EXIST. TODAY, THEY HAVE TRIED EVERYTHING TO RAISE YOU ALL AGAINST YOUR REFORMIST, PROGRESSIST, BUILDER, ARCHITECT AND FERVENT COMPATRIOT DONALD TRUMP. HOWEVER, WHAT I KNOW FOR SURE, IN 2029, WHEN I WILL BE LEAVING OFFICE, YOU WILL CRY AND WILL REGRET THAT

TRUMP'S REIGN PASSED TOO QUICKLY BECAUSE MY DREAM, AS ALWAYS, IS TO ACCOMPLISH THE MISSION THAT HAS BEEN TRUSTED TO ME, THAT OF LEAVING AN UNFORGETTABLE SOUVENIR IN THE MEMORY OF ALL AMERICANS, NAMELY: DONALD J. TRUMP WAS THE BEST AND THE GREATEST PRESIDENT OF THE COUNTRY ON EARTH, THE UNITED STATES OF AMERICA. AND THIS, IN ALL, ECONOMY, SECURITY, SOCIAL, POLITICS, AND EDUCATION TERMS."

Although his everlasting opponents, especially his own so-called friends and collaborators of the same political party, have become crazy, blind, and deaf to ignore that, as the Latin expression says, "Vox populi, vox Dei." Instead of seeing that Trump is the actual revelation and that he's untouchable, unavoidable, unstoppable, and unbeatable, they saw fit to add fuel to the fire lit by Joe Biden and his liberal Democrats. They are also sick of power; they are comparable to a bicycle without brakes, a starless sky for not wanting to know and understand despite winds and tides. Trump's supporters and voters will not move an inch to go shopping elsewhere. They are finally so greedy for the White House that they do not know that only Trump will be able to make them a place at the helm of business in 2029 after the good governance of the latter during 2025. But it is sad, bizarre, disgraceful, and childish in matters of political strategy and diplomacy not to know it, these traditional Republican mafia.

In this context of ideas, Trump's fans exclaim together: "Where are these wild beefs and ducks? Here we go again! Don't worry Georgia, Arizona, Las Vegas, Ohio, Wisconsin, Pennsylvania, Michigan, Florida! They're all present, right here at the bottom of the plot against Donald Trump."

Don't worry! Dr. Builder Donald Trump!

Where are they, these caressing hypocrites, chameleons, and cow's excrements whose exterior seems dry while the inside is quite damp, not to say really wet and humid. Don't worry about MAGA's fans. We are just waiting for the "D" day to peacefully give them their change back in polling stations, that of going in droves to vote Donald Trump massively by hundreds of thousands in 2024.

In fact, just as the brain seller Mark Levin would have asked, "Where did they come from to attack TRUMP? Why have they become pitiless and so wild to him?" As he said recently, "I have my own reason to not be a politician because it is a dirty duty! Outsiders that you support and give jobs, they are the first ones to be against you. For them, recognition in politics is cowardly."

By the way, the response to all these questions is quite simple, namely: These Trump's detractors, and I quote, Mike Pence, Nikki Haley, Ron DeSantis, Chris Christie, are well counted but miscalculated because the 80 million+ American voters trust, admire, and adore their charismatic leader DONALD TRUMP. They have already chosen him as their personal "CHOUCHOU" (IDOL).

As simple as that! They just trust him, the leader of MAGA, and will always remain faithful to him even when he should be behind bars in concert with his fellow Democrats who abused and mistreated him with diatribes and slander. But despite all these indifference signs against Trump, they still try to parody him to build their sense of humor, between them, Chris Christie! In this context, Donald Trump had schooled! Don't you remember that during the second Republican debate, this same troublemaker, anti-Trump, Mister Chris by excellence tried to serve his 2016 style during a similar primary debate to say to an opponent: "Put your hand down, we still have enough time left!" In this sense, big Chris tried to parody Trump in order to at least obtain a little attention from the audience. But the problem is that Chris is far away from being of the caliber of Donald Trump in this field, because being funny and charismatic is not something that one can purchase from a supermarket or a grocery store. It's preferably a donation from beyond with which Trump was already born. As a result, the audience didn't pay any attention to his joke, not to say turn deaf and blindfold.

By the way, let's change the phase of the subject. After all the irrefutable proof of the bad governance of Biden with an economy in disarray, a border crisis without limit, a high cost of living making the middle and lower class more vulnerable. What about the dizzying rise in fuel price causing hundreds of thousands of people to store their car in the garage, a startled awakening was expected of all Republican leaders to behave like harmless serpents and doves to say to Trump, "listen, this time we are going very vigilant to avoid falling into the traps and false accusations of leftists. We will unite together to bring corrections to his poltroon attitude towards our international opponents and also his policy of sloppiness bequeathed to this country as a diabolical heritage." Unfortunately, once again it is the contrary that is occurring for opting to work instead as Satan in a disobedience mind animated by hatred to be against Donald Trump.

Is it too late for them to still be as wise as serpents and harmless as those doves? Is it still too late for them to pack up and turn back to board the MAGA Caravan? Oh, no! But not at all! It's never too late to do well.

To repeat the old adage, great things are not always necessary to deserve esteem. All our fellow lost sheep must do is to only tempt them, these things in question, and they will still be welcome home by the Architect of MAGA because, DONALD TRUMP is always for the union making us what we are today.

By the way, since passion in whatever form it presents is always contrary to reason, they may still be tenacious in turning a deaf ear and believing only when they see clearly. However, this enthusiastic demonstration, postered by MAGA supporters in front of the justice court in Miami recently, sent them a sharp and clear message: America and Trump first! What about a poll found on the same day of his appearance in court, where 91% of Republicans want to stay faithful and vote for Trump? Also, we thought that only through cinematographic films that we can see: Alone beats All.

With Donald Trump, it is not necessarily true, then the latter who makes headlines. Are we not face to face with reality? 71% in his favor while only 29% remain ingredients to be shared with more than seven other candidates! Woah! Doesn't that mean anything to them?

Anyway, as the other said: Someone who is not patient is like a lamp without oil because it is the only way towards success. In this context, don't be afraid! A little patience is required, and we will see that everything will be fixed after evidence has managed to testify to the veracity of the facts and find the great ARCHITECT OF MAGA INNOCENT.

Therefore, the question arises, what is the law? The law is not all the PhDs, Master's degrees acquired in the most reputable universities in the world! The law is a matter of common sense and conscience! Without these two legitimate factors, all these will not serve you. You will not also be capable of shedding the light to give justice to whom it is due! In this sense, as a real novice in this field, as it is often said, with a lot of juries, a simple recap of TRUMP's past in the face of his tough opponents from 2015 to the present day will be enough to detect the truth from the false.

Do juries need to be experts in this domain to decide? The jury must be able to appeal to their good sense and conscience to say in a unanimous way that we are not worth going where Joe Biden and his acolytes want us to go. More than twenty false accusations, two erroneous impeachments, and several other calumnies during the first term of a president who wanted to accomplish marvelous things and change the well-being of the country for whom he was the leader.

The members of the jury must also know that even in the difficult times that the country was going through during China's COVID-19, Trump was treated as a divisive leader, not to say a pet peeve black bird who wanted to implant a policy of racism and hatred all over the world, especially towards China when the latter accused them of being the main instigator of the spread of COVID-19 and that from now on, air flights from China to all US territories are prohibited until further notice. What such a magnanimous, protective, and patriotic decision! Unfortunately condemned by the left and politicians, country sellers.

How do they actually feel when faced with the reality of the facts? Why not lay a mea culpa on the American people for having misled them by calling Trump a failure, falterer, and a troublemaker dangerous and annoying for the country? A president who tried to do everything in his strength and power. A president who tried to fight hard to discover a rapid vaccine in record time for this infernal pandemic fomented by CHINA.

Instead of encouraging him, the liberal leftists went way back to antiquity to say that it is impossible to find a suitable vaccine in such a short period of time because, with Polio, HIV, and others, it has always taken more than three or five years to find a real vaccine to materialize the pandemic. But what they don't know, either by malice or stupidity, is that science has well evolved!

Furthermore, the Bible says: for everything, there is a time. Didn't they know it? A simple example is enough to testify to the veracity. In the past, when one suffered from a headache, we quickly went to a clinic to find out where this symptom came from.

At the present time, it can be easily remedied by asking Google!

Can we really talk about him without knowing his socio-political and economic background? Donald Trump is an encyclopedia, well open to everyone to read and learn. What you read in the introduction is what you will read again in the conclusion. Many say that politics are made of promises, but not really actions. Maybe that is why he has always said that he's not a politician. Donald is someone who can respect his words. You could see during his leadership, he hired a lot of anti-Trumpists and gave them the highest executive posts, such as Secretary of State of Foreign Affairs, Department of Justice, to only name these two. However, referring ourselves through different opinions issued by the appointees named above, they criticized Trump worse than his Democrat opponents. This is what is called in the dictatorial language: recognition is cowardly, Mr. Trump!

Donald Trump was and will always be the president of every single American living in the interior of the country and overseas. Don't forget his password: America first! There is no question of Black, Latino, Asian American, etc.

BY THE WAY, FOR YOUR COMPREHENSION AND YOUR MEMORY, WHO IS DONALD TRUMP?

He Builder, Architect, Reformist, and Revolutionary of the Party.

Donald was born on June 14, 1946, in QUEENS, NEW YORK. Without wishing to elaborate at length and breadth on his family since Trump is an open book to the American people, I would like to say only that he came from a very hardworking, ambitious, and disciplined family.

The Trump family is so vast in the history of great educational and economic success, that it could take all eternity to talk about them and detail them point by point for the edification and understanding of the world, more especially the American people. A family of five children called 5 out of 5, which is equal success on all angles, namely: Pilot of Career, Bank Executive, etc., to lead to Donald Trump, the Architect of the family. From these laurels collected both in terms of professionalism, education, and economy, we are unanimous in recognizing that it is a family very flattered and proud to contribute to the immense emancipation and progress accomplished for their country. 5 out of 5! Wherever Mr. Fred Trump is actually, beyond of course, he must be very happy with the success of his children to certify that he did not waste his time for having provided a careful education to his children, with Donald Trump the Avant-Garde.

By the way, biblically speaking, it seems that Trump is well and truly protected by the universe for having meticulously applied the fifth commandment of God, formulating that the child of God must honor and respect his mother and his father. From this perspective, we would tend to see a Donald Trump who has become a servile imitator to follow step by step his father's trajectory, continuing his duty and expertise to reach the climax. To illustrate this, two examples suffice. First, Trump is a real estate builder. Secondly, just like his dad, he is also a father of five children; this is really called: like father, like son.

Do we not see that Donald Trump, despite winds and human tides, always emerged victorious? His detractors are far from being divine certainty that they continue to prosecute a man who has all the beyond protections. They have become true devils to forget that even when they try to propose to impose themselves, it is always up to the Lord to have the final word and dispose.

How did the Trump Family emerge to carve out a prominent and secure place, giving work to thousands of Americans? Fred Trump was not born rich. He lived in the Bronx, New York! When it has become a much vulnerable city currently, the Bronx has still not a city inhabited by the privileged class and most of the middle class. Mr. Fred only acquired a high school diploma, except a diploma like that is not as high level. All to say that Trump, Dad was not opulent overnight.

In this context, knowing there is never no stupid job, but a lot of stupid people, Fred Trump started out like a plumber and eventually got into building and repairing homes to help this family become what it is today. Thus instead of discrimination and racism, it was necessary to explain to people that the Trump fortune was not realized through bad deals either in Ukraine, China, Romania, Russia, to only name these countries. This fortune was the result of a long journey of a colossal effort for the concretization of the American Dream.

On this, we are always pleased with the opinion of the great black American actor, Denzel Washington, for when he has a chance to elaborate on this subject, educates his compatriots in this regard. On the contrary, the success of the Trumps would have served as a great example to the American people to follow the same trajectory to know the path to success.

WHO IS REALLY TRUMP'S FAMILY, THEIR ROOTS, THEIR PASS AND SO ON?

It was a wonderful morning on June 15, 1946, when the couple, Fred Trump and his wife, Mary Anne MacLeod, gave birth to their fourth child in Queens Hospital, New York City, bearing the name of Donald J. Trump.

As we always say, like father, like son. One would say that since he was in his mother's womb, he was already born a builder, a genius in the area of construction, for a job that was always well planned and successful. Even when he parodied his father to become who he is these days, Donald Trump was already cherishing the dream to surpass his dad in this area because he said, for there to be evolution, the son must get ahead of the father. If his dad was a foreman and real estate broker, don't be surprised that Fred Trump was also a plumber of circumstances. He was not well off!

As a versatile person, he did not bother to undertake those types of works in his own apartments for rent, which without any doubt allowed him, of course, to make a lot of savings by spending less.

Regarding Donald Trump and speaking of evolution, as soon as he obtained his Bachelor of Science in Economics from the Wharton School of the University of Pennsylvania in 1968, in concert with his dad, Fred, he began to work tirelessly to gain a place, just like him.

A leading place, of course, in the most titled country, great capitalist of the world (USA). This is how already, as President Manager for the Trump Organization at only 25 years old, we were already dealing with a multi-millionaire Donald J. Trump. A bright young star who never since then stopped shining and became well known throughout the United States as well as the whole planet. So on this point, we pause a little to elaborate more.

In this sense, it is from there we could greatly establish the difference between Donald Trump and so-called black leaders who, apparently speaking, often claim to be fierce defenders of this disadvantaged and neglected layer. But yet deep down, it is always the opposite which often makes the result vivid in the eyes of everyone.

That said, from the first day that Donald Trump was gratified by his dad, he only had one dream in mind, that of creating mass jobs for hundreds of American people who were short of wages. But as for those criticizing him severely and bitterly, what are they doing with exorbitant hundreds of millions collected after multiple speeches and massive sales of their memoir? Have they used at least a minimum of those millions to reduce the unemployment rate among the latter of whom they claim to be fervent defenders and representatives? Don't they know full well that they are still at the bottom of the table as was the case during their first community service experiences in matters of employment in Chicago? Do they have short memories so as not to remember it? Fortunately, thanks so much to God for giving strength to their brothers and sisters in the Black American Independent Media who, in the majority, have rung the alarm bell allowing this neglected and flouted layer in question to finally wake up to say no to the pleasant, flattering, lame words and false promises every four years before presidential elections.

Thus, because of the accurate and conscientious mediatic work of education, the latter has become capable of seeing crystal clear to detect the true from the false. They want concrete and verified actions! Don't you dare tell us, brother-sister, what you're going to do for us in 2024! But preferably, tell us what you did well for your so-called brothers and sisters twelve years ago during your presidential dolls, extravaganza, and joke in Washington DC! If this question doesn't deserve a prompt and adequate response, please know from now on, we are totally divorced from DEMAGOGUERY!

To return to Donald Trump, knowing well that there is not necessarily a single path leading to Rome, he seized the opportunity to convert himself into a backyard bird to fly on all the branches. This is how he found himself apart from the Real Estate Builder, but also as Boxing's Promoter, Entertainer, Organizer of the Beauty Pageant, and TV Personality.

However, describing politics as a dirty duty and also knowing that everything has its time, Donald Trump had never interfered in politics during his era as a professional businessman so as not to deviate from his trajectory toward the path of progress he had already set his sights on for a perfectly successful future in this field.

Despite everything, he always supported community and political activities without being able to claim anything in return, as much as he has always said: UNITED STATES first! Such is Donald Trump's slogan all the time.

Under this context of ideas, he very closely observed the attitude of political leaders to have an overall idea of it. Thus, after a long observation of the way politicians wanting to tarnish the image of the United States to transform this great country titled Paradise on Earth into a Banana Republic, he finally decided to make spectacular breakthroughs to ensure the defense of the voiceless so that the dream of every single American in this country does not fall by the wayside and into the garbage, but is well concretized.

It is not without reason that he has been the object of intimidation and persecution because he chose to help the weakest in America. Although, it's not a big problem for

Donald Trump. He doesn't mind! He always quotes: LET PERISH THE MORIBUND SYSTEM!

Because it is sometimes good to delay on the way, but finally bring the good news. Actually, we are facing the reality of the facts! This question of discrimination and racism doesn't stand, especially with technology, which has allowed everyone to identify the true face of the demagogues, troublemakers, and left political activists to slander and destroy the reputation of the Trump family who loves this country so much, ignoring the origins of the latter to take aim at such courageous workers whose vocation is to create jobs to contribute to the security, beauty, and success of the country. They just speculate without taking the time to understand and educate people that Trump's Mom and Dad were not drawn from the elite nor New York bourgeoisie. Instead, they were from either middle-class or hardworking people!

However, with the desire to move forward, they worked courageously and tirelessly to carve out such a place in this American society, and they are proud of it. To testify to this, did you know that Donald Trump's mother, Mrs. Mary Anne MacLeod Trump's first job in New York was daycare? Did you also know that Mr. Fred Trump only had a High School Diploma Degree? But during that time, Harvard, Yale, and Columbia University already existed! Reverend Martin Luther King Jr., President George H. Bush, to name a few, were respectively part of those graduates. However, Fred Trump would have seemed too from the same generation!

The question to ask: why did he only and simply hold a High School Diploma, when in the eyes of everyone knowing him, especially undoubtedly his preferred son Donald J. Trump, a brilliant, smart, and intelligent young adult? So, in this erroneous context to make them the object of all bad names had been bitter, partial, and very malicious to them.

Today, it has become the time where the American people, especially Black African-Americans, to wake up and start opening their eyes wide to say loudly that we were totally mistaken and deceived because Trump is one of the rare American leaders who recognizes and admits for true that the Black African-Americans were the ones largely to build this country. Thus, as a reward, Donald Trump vowed to work hard to be grateful to them. Then they understand it well. As a result, according to several surveys, it is for the first time in American history that a strong percentage of blacks registered to vote in droves for a Republican President, Donald Trump. So far, on a year of the D-day, the percentage of blacks registered to vote for Trump is phenomenal and unbelievable. Again, at one year of the "D" day, the percentage has already reached 23%.

What do we also say about Latino voters? The number has been increasing considerably; that is to say, approximately 50% have already agreed to take the road with Donald J. Trump in the 2024 electoral votes. And the latter is already very grateful. Once again, to repeat after the old adage, it is sometimes good to be late, but bring good news.

Today, with Donald Trump all fire, all flame, we are currently facing the reality of the facts. It took time; therefore, the message is finally received and understood. This also means that when the cat is out of the bag, all the hidden secrets are discovered and revealed. No more discrimination and barriers of race and color in it. Of course, it might play a role in it, but not for those who have a full and well-rounded head. More specifically, Black-African Americans and Latinos who know well what speaking means. In this sense, their message against the left activist demagogue democrats is crystal clear.

Today, if you consider it as arrogance because we are fighting for a better future, that is your full right. However, being able to finally be wise and very educated to detect your political games, drunk hypocrisy, and demagoguery, we are all, black minority Latinos, revolted to no longer tolerate that for being just like you, men and women of this entity with full and well-rounded heads. Today again, the polite game is worth it. As a result, Trump will be the main winner. Let's elaborate and be more explicit! We said above that all secrets are currently revealed. It's not without reason! It took time for people to understand Trump's strong character, his personality, and his commitments to achieve good deeds. All this ultimately has convinced American people to admit that he makes a big difference in the present time.

Do you know that between the last six Presidents of the United States, he's the only one on the list who took the oath already very rich, while showing a very negative balance of his fortune after his mandate? For him, it's not all serious because he sees the presidency as being an honorary title to serve the nation well and save it from the clutches of overseas enemies and unpatriotic local oligarchs. It's not a business to reap the country.

However, unlike many others of the latter, what matters most to Donald Trump is above all his patriotic feeling for the country. It is also a depth of thoughts nourished by great dreams for an ever powerful, correct, and respectful UNITED STATES OF AMERICA.

So, speaking of these Presidents in question who increased their fortune after the end of their mandate, we begin with President Ronald Reagan 1981-1989. His fortune increased from 10.6 million dollars to 16.4 million. George H. Bush 1989-1993, his wealth had passed from 4 million to 23 million dollars.

Bill Clinton, 1993-2001. As an ex-governor of a small State, which is Arkansas where, contrary to the great ones like New York, the salary of Bill was not quite Catholic, whether only 35 thousand dollars a year then, including some untenable fees and benefits. Just to say that a Governor in the State of Arkansas is the least paid compared to the other 49 remaining states. But despite all, that did not prevent Bill from subscribing to the list of the multimillionaires in this country. Therefore, it was only 1.3 million from 1981 to 1992 as governor. But as president from 1993 to 2001, according to the media sources, we would have seen that this net worth of 1-3 million dollars was going to speed up quite exaggeratedly to reach out to 135-4 million! Such a last rough hour flash news had just plunged the media, especially that of the minority, to ask a lot of questions, namely:

Why spend all a Cathedral of times to become, Lawyers, Doctors, Architects of profession when being politicians you can like him transform a goat network into an elephant's one? On this point, one might say that the IRS fails to do its duty! As far as Obama, he seems to be very brilliant and smart. One also said of him that he's a brain-seller. He would only accept checks for his books, which hit a record in this field. Regarding other illegal transactions, if there would have been, it will be going to be ultra difficult to accredit him just like we do to his former vice-president given that there's no checks issued in his name!

What about George W. Bush, 2001-2009? His net worth, which totaled a balance of 20 million dollars, has doubled after the term of his mandate to 40 million.

Regarding President Barack Hussein Obama, to repeat after Rush Limbaugh, from 2001 to 2009, his fortune, just like Bill Clinton's, has known a sensational peak, starting at 1-3 million in 2009 to reach a colossal sum of 70 million dollars after the end of his mandate in 2017. However, for many of the reasons noted above, in case the jealousies or madness of the IRS for some reason, would push to question the fortune of the mixed-blood ex-president, the latter would have no problem proving that his Mega Fortune has come directly from the sweat of his brow through titanic work as a brain-seller! Can one be also optimistic concerning the other?

President Biden, although not yet finishing his only one term, must not be excluded from the list because he too made his cheese there!

So, in 2010, after being a senator for almost 40 years, Joe Biden's net worth was only $228,012. As Vice-President from this said year to present, his fortune is valued at $10 million. Therefore, further, you will notice that his fortune was $1.5 million before taking office to be actually estimated at $9.5 million actually.

The same source has made believe that, contrary to rumors of bad deals with foreign instances and shenanigans of all kinds, the President made his profit through real estate, several speeches, books, etc. Finally, Trump is the only main loser of the G7 game, if one can call it that!

From 2017 to 2021, President Trump's net worth has considerably diminished. A part of China's COVID-19, including impeachments, indictments of all kinds. Donald Trump's fortune was $4.5 billion when he took the oath in 2017. Currently, his net worth is evaluated at $2.5 billion. In fact, a deficit total of $2 billion. And despite all of the above, he's still proud of it.

It is in this context that the majority of the American people have just discovered in Donald Trump someone who talks and acts. What so-called, promises made, promises kept. Despite all these stories, it appears that a bit of light has just emerged to illuminate the lanterns of the people who lost their way by saying: if these misers in question are really democrats in principle. If they are really conscious and concerned, why not revive and put into practice the historical thinking of JFK, namely: "Never ask what your country can do for you. But preferably, ask what you can do for your country." Yet, Donald Trump is not a democrat! Therefore, that doesn't prevent him from using this magnanimous JFK's declaration to always apply it point-blank! But as other entities on the other side, who are commonly called speakers, they only have one option in mind, that of loudly talking and filling their pockets, but so as not to give anything in return to the channel of the voiceless, which they always use to convey their political ambitions and shenanigans every four years when it is a question of elections!

So, it's not without reason that many Americans, to the disappointment of corrupt oligarchic elites, have ended up taking into account and recognizing as true the latter's dream for the USA. At the same time, all the new and old arrivals taking place at MAGA's board consider Trump as a brilliant sun who shines every day compared to his opponents on the other side who are described as a dark moon under the influence of fog all night long, groping through a sky remaining starless.

DONALD TRUMP'S ECONOMIC JOURNEY

Trump believes in the evolution of things. His philosophy dictates that in order to speak of evolution, the student must be able to surpass his teacher. He observed his dad hire hundreds of workers in his construction projects for decades. How not to extend it and provide more jobs for Americans?

It is in this sense, although the construction of an avalanche of buildings in the heart of the world's capital, New York City, his ambition did push him to explore LAS VEGAS and, more precisely, ATLANTIC CITY, NEW JERSEY. Donald Trump created employment for 8,000 workers by building three international casino-hotels and entertainments, which brought considerable income to the city.

With the presence of Donald Trump in Atlantic City, a small town, it was the joy of living in the hearts of all the residents in this town to find something good to do because 8,000 people hired by only Donald Trump for a city of 40,560 inhabitants then, was not a small task. It was with reason ATLANTIC CITY was called the LAS VEGAS OF NEW JERSEY, where tourists did not trade their presence as long as they enjoyed the sidewalk, the beautiful sand of the beach, and the musical-sport atmosphere, including restaurants and entertainments. As for boxing competitions, Trump Plaza had almost made Madison Square Garden forgotten as it was solicited by national-international flights.

Unfortunately, everything was supposed to fall apart by a liberal policy of letting each other sprout to set up casinos here and there, that is to say: Philadelphia, Pennsylvania, NEW YORK CITY, Connecticut, and all these surroundings. Also, 9/11 weighs heavily on New York, affecting almost the entire world, without forgetting this thoughtless invasion in Iraq, plunging the country into an unprecedented economic disaster.

It is from this unfortunate invasion in question, we would recognize the true face of Donald Trump. In the meantime, to go back to our topic, since then, we did observe and see a destitute Atlantic City in a state of degradation to become more vulnerable under the banner of Governor Chris Christie in 2015 when the city had a record unemployment rate of 15.5%. But despite this poor performance, this power freak had the audacity to run for the presidency of the United States in that same catastrophic and crucial period, including his famous BRIDGE GATE, from which he came out safe and sound because of the current practice of the justice called, "THE REASON OF THE STRONGEST IS ALWAYS THE BEST."

In this sense, Trump looked Chris straight in the eye and said, "What good things do you think you can promise?"

BREAKTHROUGH AND POLITICAL CAREER OF DONALD TRUMP

The reason why Donald Trump was always conceived as an outsider is because he would have considered politics as not only a science but also an expression of wisdom, which claims to be patient. For Trump, it would seem that getting involved and noticed quickly without firing a shot would be an option doomed to failure, especially when you are already in such a business domain which is quite different from politics. However, Trump's philosophy would have also dictated to him, politics with either money or political affiliation and experience is again a perilous trajectory leading to a premature fiasco not to easily resurface on the scene. And if the manner to act that way was not our imagination, but really his, we might admit he was already a genius in this domain.

During all this time, he dedicated his time to creating jobs by being like his father, an entrepreneur. Moreover, at only 25 years of age, he was already the principal manager of his father's real estate company.

"It's little by little the bird builds his nest," we often say, don't we?

According to Trump's concept, you don't start two things at once because everything has its time. A time to focus on work, a time to indulge in politics. Moreover, from the fruits harvested from the work, which allow you to reinforce political assets and advantages over other opponents. Thus, through traditional debates, you must expect such questions, namely: What have you already accomplished in your political career to get people to vote for you?

We are sure and certain that if such a question was in the honor to be part of the debate in 2020 to allow voters to have an idea of Joe Biden to know with whom they will be dealing, according to his negative record of old date in the senate, the latter would either remain speechless or push his audacity as usual by shooting aside.

However, through all the imaginable and unimaginable reflections on Donald Trump to grasp the depths of his political ideology or at least the real objective he has set for the revolution titled: AMERICANISM, with which, he was going to do everything he could to walk without getting tired to allow this political ideology to take off like an eagle flying to destiny in 2015. But several people would ask the big question; Where has Donald Trump been all this time? Was he, like a little serpent growing under a rock? Whatever the way you interpret his fighting tactic, he's right for having always lived in New York City, not only the Capital of the World but also principal of mafia where any time your ideas, projects, and secrets can be exposed in the blink of an eye to divert you and send you to the butcher.

If we analyze it well and also understand it well the manner to well monitor a situation, once again Trump must be delighted for being more realistic rather than idealistic. Anyway, the slowness and the reluctance of Donald Trump before his spectacular breakthrough and his triumphant entry into the American political scene deserve to be appreciated for being an outspoken politician without, like other traditional politicians, obtaining a PhD in this field. It was really smart of him acting that way. It is called, the natural prevails over the superficial. In fact, if even despite his maturity currently speaking, he's still considered like a lamb surrounded by graybeard lions. What if it was long before he was barely making his appearance in this realm? It would go from bad to worse.

Donald J. Trump, although a book well open in the eye of everyone, it is still difficult without a well-rested head to go straight to the point talking openly about his political strategy, especially since he occupies a role of versatility if we allow ourselves, this way of speaking, to be everywhere on the field to find a way to score big. In this sense, we do observe sometimes, once he was armed with his shot, we thought he was going directly from a distance. Finally, instead, he passes the ball, and this, vice-versa. In this perspective of ideas, it would be better to follow him step by step. Avoiding kicking him with red bullets to not induce people in errors.

We said before that everything has its time. Trump seemed, although always busy taking care of businesses, used his spare time to read and learn a lot from experienced leaders, especially those from overseas to enrich his political experience and make his way in this field.

As a result, we are trying to go back to the French colonial era to appeal to a genius nicknamed the little BLACK JACOBIN from whom we could find a similarity towards the image and political trajectory of DONALD TRUMP. This one, speaking of the little Black Jacobin, had to take time to study deeply the bad and good side of each of the colonizing countries, such as France, England, and Spain to know precisely in which camp to stay. Finally, he chose to line up on the side of the French, which by the general proclamation of the emancipation of the slaves allowed (little Jacobin), Toussaint Louverture to see that alone in the company of the latter, he would be able to defray the chronicle and win the case realizing his dream for the forgotten men and women commonly called the voice of voiceless.

Thus, just like him (T. Louverture), we saw a Donald Trump who, for his first appearance in 1987 on the political scene, wore his Republican Hat. Once again, why was he waiting so long when we all know that he was already a well-responsible citizen; a progressive Manager-entrepreneur of

41 years old in 1987? What explains this slowness to fulfill his civic duty? Does registering at the age of 41 mean he started voting at that age? If so, how to explain it for the full comprehension of the readers?

Far from being a historian to relate proven facts ranging from the period 1963 to 1981, we were inclined to notice that politically speaking, the country was not doing well. We understood each other well and were about to explain why everything was going wrong.

It was no secret that this period was a heavy blow for the United States. This crisis was so shocking that it would tend to plunge the country into total anarchy that took your breath away. And for all this, the whole world remained perplexed to ask the question: What's going on with this country considered the band leader and the champion of the world?

Therefore, it was no doubt a whole avalanche of socio-political crises that made a splash there. Starting with the problems of racism and discrimination to prohibiting access to the front seat in a bus to blacks (1962-1963), passing through the filthy and cowardly assassination of President F.J. Kennedy, including his brother Robert, very intellect, a brain seller, but liberal (1963-1968), without also forgetting the assassination of the famous black leader, competent and serious, Dr. Martin Luther King Jr. That should not always be compared to Jesse and Al, to only name a few. What about the Watergate scandal putting President Richard Nixon upside down in his little shoes in 1973? To finally lead to Jimmy Carter, a super and ultra champion liberal of the practice of sloppiness and grumbling policy plunging the United States into an economic-diplomatic slump to never forget, 1977-1981.

But it is very unfortunate for the country to see that more than forty years after, his roots are about to grow greater again with his servile imitator, President Joe Biden who wishes to beat his record not too far away.

Now, after long recourse in this period of political pandemic that the country was going through, one could get an idea of Trump's sign of reluctance to shine brightly in abstention. In fact, analyzing the political journey of the two politician leaders, namely, Toussaint Louverture (little black Jacobin) to whom we attribute a certain similarity to Donald Trump, given the way they managed to breakthrough far and wide on the political scene, thus comes spontaneously a coincidence perhaps from beyond because when the vol deface of each of them is observed, Toussaint and Trump sought by all means to find out where there is weakness on the side of the enemies to take advantage of it, gain also the upper hand and fill the void.

For this, we deduce that it is really extraordinary tactics in terms of making the right recipe in politics. Therefore, the only two differences we can establish between these two leaders are that Toussaint learned to read at 33 years old while Trump did when he was only 5 or 6 years old. Furthermore, Toussaint's soldiers and partisans were always very loyal to him, while Trump, although his desire to collaborate well with his friends is often betrayed by most of them.

To get an idea of their strategy, Toussaint had started with Spain, passing through England to definitely stay with France where he found the great opportunity to proclaim himself Governor General of the whole country. As far as Donald Trump, he went to the Republican camp in 1987.

In 1999, he integrated the Reformist Party. In 2001, he had changed his tune to squarely press his luck with the Democrats, which is the most difficult one where there were too many gray-bearded, selfish, and ambitious candidates, sometimes for only one post.

In 2009 to the present, he returned to the fold to finally beat Hillary Clinton masterfully and democratically. Wow! What started creating a situation of panic through the streets of certain liberal states for more than two weeks in November 2016, especially in New York where all fans and many others occupied the street in droves in protest after this victory in the apotheosis of Donald Trump over the former Obama's right hand, Hillary Clinton. The entire world cried bitterly to say: What kind of democracy are democrats talking about? How to camp on the cross to rise up against a President religiously and democratically elected by the Vox Populi, Vox Dei?

We don't know for sure if the famous American Super Star, Madonna had been promised either a ministerial post in Hillary's cabinet or at least she would seem to have invested a lot on the last to win that she assumed the right to say with rage that she's ready to set the White House on fire if Trump dares to swear in on JANUARY 18, 2017. Ultimately, President Obama, covered with sadness and shame, finally intervened to say: That is too much! Prophet Abraham says: Enough is Enough!

We are a democratic country. May the best win! May calm return to the streets and homes!

Even though a little bit tardive, it deserved to be appreciated. Also, by this gesture from his part, I can say that I was not totally deceived. At least, I got something in return from all my support for the latter.

SLIDING TACKLES AND BOSSY PLAY

Just like in love, we often say that pleasant words are its main food; the same is true for politics, namely: sweetheart and flattering words are what make voters walk. However, in any rule, there are always exceptions. Nevertheless, without bragging about it and inventing this exception, wanting to stay in the realm of the facts, DONALD TRUMP, if we can say so, is so far the unique political leader who has been able to keep his election campaign promises.

Yes, we can say it loudly and repeat it in all frankness: Trump made an exception to this traditional rule, not to say false promises but to act accurately. He had well and truly proven it in the eyes of all Americans during his 2017-2021 mandate. This is called, promises done, promises kept.

It's not without reason that Trump says he's not a politician because politics is not straight, politics is hypocrisy and dirty duty. It was not a small task to govern a country while surrounded by people who only care about their own pocket, not the country. Although his skills, his determination, his experience watching religiously all mistakes committed by his predecessors trying to correct them rapidly to M-A-G-A, the left and most of his colleagues in the party also don't want Trump to Americanize the country. For them, globalization is the best option for the United States of America, then, by which, it will always create for them a gateway which will allow them to swim more in corruption to earn their hundreds of millions much more easily outside of constitutional norms.

Trump is not strong enough to assume such a responsibility alone. He needs support from serious and competent compatriots to end globalization and replace it with Americanization, which is excellent for M-A-G-A.

Therefore, it's not without reason that a ministerial cabinet with serious and competent people was previously either suggested or proposed to Donald Trump to lead on good governance and excellent performance in 2025.

Among other things, people must know that Americanization does not mean division, racism, and discrimination just as many leftists would have a tendency to misinterpret it. It means to be proud of your country. It also means working for the progress and the prosperity of the country by serving it with loyalty and pride to keep it safe and sound as always the number one on earth.

That is the principal reason that excited me to have a preference for Donald Trump, seeing him as someone feeling a sentiment of pure love for the USA because I have been raised in a country where people are careless while consequences are grave and result in the balance sheet super negative. How do you not appreciate Donald Trump, when he says: AMERICA FIRST!!!

As we said before, Americans have always been a respected nation. American people used to be considered the most courteous and generous people.

Why? Is it because Americans are the most good-looking people? No and No! However, money always talks! With their greens, they don't give a s*it about the Pope in the Vatican!

Erotically speaking, statistics have revealed that 99.99% of overseas women look for American men!

Why? Because this is where the water runs cooler! Don't our leaders know about it?

Why do hundreds of thousands want to settle in the USA? Because they believe it is the only earthly paradise where they could always make the right recipe and harvest. Don't our morons and patrons' leaders know about it?

What should happen when we let ourselves be induced in error by the left to be out of this avant-garde factor, going broke and losing all these appreciations and admiration of other nations?

Americans must understand and not tolerate any question of discrimination and racism. They play the same brutal game when it is a matter of election. They send you a black leader to create polemics of color and discrimination to make you believe they are the only solution.

Therefore, you're not from BANANA REPUBLICS. You must take a deep breath to say: How much did I used to spend on food and fuel, to only name a few, in 2018, 2020 compared to now? How much money did I save under Trump's administration compared to now?

In this sense, you should be able to establish the difference between false and true leaders.

VICTIMS OF DISCRIMINATION

Contrary to the media, which paint Donald Trump in all imaginable colors in regard to discrimination, the latter is more victimized than anybody else. They criticized him for not being intellectual. I was very surprised to hear people say that Donald Trump is stupid. For these people, being intellectual means holding a PhD in political science either at Harvard or Yale University, to only name these two. However, they no longer took into account a young Entrepreneur-Architect who, already at only 25 years of age, was carving out a place in American society.

Occupying and playing a leading role in a large-scale company founded by his father, Fred Trump, Donald Trump, as the headquarters manager, was the one who designed and decided for the full success of it, and it was a job well done, allowing Donald Trump to reach the CLIMAX!

However, all did not stop there, in the beauty and architectural masterpiece. It was also necessary to wait for the great, spectacular, and triumphant breakthrough of Donald Trump, being often treated as big morons and big shoes by his detractors. Therefore, what was funny to observe as a reality is that the majority of the harsh and unfounded criticism came in majority from the low-class Americans, often forgotten, the voice of the voiceless, for whom he was going to throw himself into a big and difficult fight for relief of financial life. Thus, it was in 2016, during numerous electoral debates, people ended up realizing that they had been greatly mistaken about all the bad qualifiers attributed to Trump. All fire, all flame, Trump was armed with the file in the hands of all his opponents to become a true Historian to well refresh their memory, which was often wavered on proven facts. Trump, as a true observer and a real strategist, had to know that Jeb Bush was the one to be mistreated first in words with irrefutable proof.

Everybody knows that the war in Iraq was beneficial at all for the country because after 9/11, the Capital of the World, New York City, was in sadness where businesses had been bitterly affected. And when it is New York, it's not a small task!

It's not also without reason, the others said: any bad economic beats in New York also correspond to the pulse of the world, see the neighboring 49 States! What was even worse was the invasion of Iraq under the leadership of George W. Bush, whose brother, Jeb Bush, aspired to be the third one of the Bush family to be elected President of the United States. For this particular reason, Donald Trump was the first one to announce the color, attacking profoundly Governor Jeb Bush, tackling him severely, asking also to look straight in the eyes at American people who are the main victims by paying very expensively the consequence of an unnecessary nonsense war in Iraq.

Jeb Bush must know that like the man who does not live on bread alone, it is the same that the man does not live only on war. Your father had done it, your brother just recently came to do it in Iraq. As far as you, Governor Jeb, are you a candidate to reiterate these same things? Among other things, didn't you know that this consequential expensive invasion was wanted, heard, and planned by your brother and close entourage?

Today, in the name of the forgotten men and women, the voice of the voiceless, I shall be delighted that you answer this question because if you love American people and the country, you must have the courage to tell them the truth.

Furthermore, are you aware of what costing our country went through in this sense? More than 13 trillion dollars! The shameful war in Iraq registered casualties exceeding 3,400, hostile deaths evaluated at 800, while over 31,000 troops were wounded in action. A very cheeky question that transformed the color of Governor Jeb's skin into a real super ripe tomato. A simple question that Jeb Bush had great difficulty answering, preferring to smile slyly, hypocritically speaking.

Well armed with proof in hand, Trump did not put water in his mouth to mince his words, proving to millions of American voters that these cats are actually out of the bags; they are caught right away in the eyes of everyone. Between these big cats, the governor was the most affected because Trump's political philosophy dictated to him to always tackle opponents the most tough and opulent, of which was Jeb Bush, the main opponent to be identified in this regard.

As a result, the latter's political boat was capsized in the open sea off Miami, Florida, never to resurface. As far as Chris Christie, the loser, seeing that his chance was quite tiny and minimal to thwart the infernal machine and unforgivable strikes of Donald Trump, he was already packing up and becoming a true ally of the latter, no doubt in search of a post of Vice-President. But what CC did not realize was that the Master who took care of Trump taught him to always opt for winning, except Chris has often been a below-average student in politics. Thus, one may be friends, perhaps an unlisted adviser. As far as Secretary of State, General Attorney, and Vice-President, you can forget them all, Chris Christie, because my name is DONALD J. TRUMP, THE WINNER, NOT CRIS C. THE LOSER! You must understand it, my friend!

Although Trump's choices were not quite Catholics, given what's going on with these guys he named to these posts, he was also right to stay away from Chris Christie's request because this guy has a face of a fox, not to say comparable to cow excrement where the top is arid while the interior is humid!

Taking into account the bitter and pungent diatribes directed against Trump, there is no doubt he was going to do the worst to betray Donald Trump in case the latter hired him to serve. It's unheard of, people say, of this CHAMELEON.

By the way, Trump was very smart not to pay any attention to Chris Christie because he did not even actually figure on the scoreboard where his percentage would have revealed less than two percent.

The other day, some benevolent correspondent told us that Chris gathered 60 people in a meeting. When he started to fire red bulls at Trump, the room was reduced to only 10 assistants. People did not hide their madness and pointed it out clearly to him, namely: "How many times must we tell you, stop talking bad about DONALD TRUMP! You hurt our feelings too, Mister Chris! We want to know what you're going to do to MAKE AMERICA GREAT AGAIN!" The recipe was so poor, one asked perplexed if he would be able to reach the first-round caucus in Iowa?

Chris was so out of his mind that he could not figure out that all the 50 people who left the meeting were Trump's voters in red.

Like Jeff, Hillary, and others, Chris will not be exempted, we can observe that he's already forgotten on the American political scene because attacking a charismatic leader of Trump's caliber it's like a boat running aground on a reef. In other words, it's destroying yourself. All this is enough to say that the author of the Bridgates is not immune to it at all.

Then came the turn of Senator Rubio and Cruz to be Trump's victims. Thus, through exchanges of fire, some more than others. However, knowing that they are from the same political party, they have also understood that politics is a balance of power.

In this sense, any contender has the right to use his or her own strategy either by pleasant words or bitter ones to make voters walk. This is called being competent Republicans guided by democratic and serious principles. In this context, criticism, despite having to always be comfortable, does not also prevent one from severely criticizing one's opponents to try to detect one's weak points and go on the attack. Therefore, since politics is and remains a relationship, it is often necessary to go through this route to convince voters and make good electoral revenue.

Nevertheless, as same-party candidates, these altercations and clashes of ideas do not owe eternal criticism. They must be temporary and remain only in the context of a campaign to know that politics is always a balance of power. We measure our strengths to know who is the strongest! Once the elections are over, and the best has won, we come together to lead the country well.

On this point, all our compliments go to Senator Marco Rubio and Ted Cruz for having well applied the principle of leading together and living well. Their spirit of understanding allowed them to quickly meditate and say: "Our Country and Republican Party First!" This is what is rightly called Competent Republicans guided by serious democratic principles. But what is quite different concerning who still hates Donald Trump to death. He's the only one who made Trump lose Pennsylvania because when Trump called Fox-News at midnight after leading Biden by 700,000 votes, Chris Christie acted as a troublemaker to bitterly criticize, namely: "Trump doesn't have any right to do so," while Biden took advantage of it. More details will be provided furthermore.

Among other things, President Trump didn't use a magic wand to predict the future. Therefore, if he did, Senator Ted Cruz would be the man he needed by his side to help him lead and defend his political agenda. It's very unfortunate that it happened like this! It's not without reason we heard him say, "I didn't know a lot of people in Washington. Actually, I do!"

Therefore, the victory for the nomination of the Republican party was one thing; however, to compete with Hillary Clinton for the conquest of the White House was another.

Fortunately, in spite of winds and tides including the interference of Russia - Russia it is said, in this electoral process to favor Donald Trump, the fervent and faithful supporters of the latter exclaimed with full throat: "LET ALL THESE DOGS BARK, WHILE OUR CARAVAN OF AMERICANISM PASSES AT FULL SPEED."

Since then, we said, no matter what, Hillary is already beaten. However, a lot of fanatics let themselves get carried away by passion, not wanting to know the political reality of their own country. What they have to know is that the elections in the United States are not solely based and relied on votes. The electorate also plays a preponderant role in this process!

The Obama-Hillary tandem, after eight years of power, thought that they were already in their oil bowl. It was not without reason that Obama, to scare voters, said there's no way that Donald Trump would be President of the United States! Anyway, don't be afraid of Trump, Hillary! After us, it will be us again!

For so long, all went crazy to minimize the value of the tall and great center forward of New York, Donald Trump, who had already technically knocked out all his opponents during the Republican primaries, and even Hillary was not exempt from it. If our memory is not short, we can remember that in one of the debates, in 2017, Hillary underestimated and diminished Trump's value before the audience said to this one: But you begged me to attend your wedding!

It is often said: Such a letter, such an answer. All to say that Trump's response clashed the entire room: But listen, Hillary, you were paid to attend; you hadn't made it free!

So, it was in 2017 when 115 million voters followed this debate. So, in statistic matters in this domain, when it comes to 11 million TV Spectators watching such an extraordinary debate, we have to multiply this number at least by 10 to know that at least 110 million that Hillary is a miser born under the zodiac sign of this vanguard factor: M-O-N-E-Y instead of that: S-C-O-R-P-I-O-N, under which she was really born.

The left was totally wrong trying by all means through polls hoisting Hillary as the real potential favorite to the general election of 2016. However, contacting people from the most affected states, such as Pennsylvania, Florida, Georgia, Arizona to name a few swing states, the opinion of people in the street sounded quite different.

Just like the way they discriminate against other people who don't agree with them, democrats neglected a lot of other swing states to only concentrate on Florida and Pennsylvania. We were quite surprised to see Hillary on three consecutive occasions visit these two states within 6 days desperately looking for the two magic numbers, 29+20, to proclaim victory and consider herself as the first female President of the United States. WOW! Counts well, but fails calculating.

To the contrary of all with hollow heads who didn't want to see and understand in order to discern the truth from the lies, it was already predicted that Hillary was going to lose. We didn't need to parody one of Biden's brothers to be crystal clear on that because a simple political and logical analysis had allowed us to discern all the truth from so many lies making us believe the Scorpion Zodiac sign was going to clash Trump with her teeth.

That is why we asked: Why all these repeated visits in PA and FL, with the presence of all these music-sport superstars on board, such as LeBron James, Bon Jovi, Beyonce-JZ, Lady Gaga, Madonna to name only those? Why also even once didn't Hillary campaign in NY, MA, CT?

The response to those questions is, first, she knew she was in trouble in those two states while feeling comfortable in these last ones. Further, too many bad records were on her file, such as: Monica Lewinsky's dossier which was still around, careless about the government documents, diplomatic failure with Kaddafi gates affair in Libya, what about Haiti where she imposed the country a cracker-gay as President while being in fifth place in the primary. As a result, it was for the first time a Republican candidate split the votes, almost fifty-fifty with a Democrat in the Haitian community of Florida.

For all those reasons, Hillary collapsed before Donald Trump. Any other trend that would lead people to believe that Hillary's defeat came from either Putin or others colluded with Donald Trump is dead wrong. Please put aside all signs of passion and fanaticism to make way for common sense to be neat and clear in order to discern the truth from the lies.

Most of us were not Trumpets before! But one sees how money makes people dirty the image of their country. Like him or not, we are obliged to love this man because he makes the difference. We don't like sitting down next to each other as friends; we like Trump because he loves the country. We would like him to always do the best he can to save the United States from being placed under the influence of China which under the Biden administration has tried on several occasions to exercise its interference, demonstrating they have the strength to announce the color in case it's necessary.

DIFFICULT PILGRIMAGE OF TRUMP IN THE FACE OF HIS ENEMIES

It was not a surprise to hear people, from the same day Trump's swearing-in, speculating through an archaic language saying that taking a snake to school is one thing, but having him sit on this same school desk is another. This is enough to make it clear that they knew what they were going to do, that of hijacking and deflecting Trump's Americanism policy to further steer the country in the right direction and progress.

Therefore, regarding the dishonesty of the Republicans to tarnish his image and prevent him from delivering his message of Americanism and making more history in this country, they make sure that the coalition is well built in order to do good and obtain a good cause over Donald Trump. All this is just to understand that Trump has been and still is victimized twice by repeated assaults from both sides. Another viewpoint would be enough, allowing us to go further to justify it, this viewpoint in question, namely: Why couldn't Trump's administration clean up the corrupt mess and diplomacy bequeathed to him by the tandem Obama-Biden, especially when one knew there were numerous, these corruptions? In this sense, without considering yourself as being a fervent lawyer representing and defending Donald

Trump, you can easily shed light to make people see crystal clear that he was badly surrounded by chameleons as collaborators.

If the Attorney General, Defense Secretary, and Foreign Affairs must be the true collaborators of the President, why did there still exist all types of shenanigans against him as much as his party controlled both Congress and Senate? Is it tangible proof testifying that Mister MAGA was truly like a lamb in a forest surrounded by wild foxes and lions? Such a narrative and comparative description has all its importance when one has observed since day one, Trumpists have never ceased to hear: Russia Russia, discrimination, prejudice, etc., they were even bitterly criticized Trump for having said: China's Covid-19!

By the way, even a Japanese girl with whom I was chatting was also against such a fact!

When I said to her, you know with China's Covid-19 everything was underwater. Thus, she replied to say, yes I know Covid-19 was terrible.

This is proof that even the country that we protect does not agree with the reality of the facts.

What is bad in the whole story is that most Republican leaders often have acted with their head, not with their brain to know that such and such things should not be done like this. Even when being sick and thirsty for power, for God's sake and country love, let's give a chance to this man to MAGA!

Instead of strengthening him when the going would get bad by showing him support and loyalty, to prevail, it is the contrary that is always the strong winds and the heavy torrential rains that interfere in the game to create situations of fear and terror resulting in making us divisive, what we are currently seeing in this country. Furthermore, as for the Democrats, they know that Fred Trump was not born a millionaire, but they refuse just to actually educate their people. But they know for sure that Trump's father only had his high school diploma. He started as a plumber. It's a question of good sense and a willingness to tell the truth. But they will never tell he was a hard and smart worker thinking of fulfilling his American dream.

Studies, colleges, and universities already existed in the UNITED STATES. Wasn't he smart enough for college or university studies? According to statistics and good performances realized, it should be a big mistake not to say a discrimination, a wickedness, and mortal sin to dare to say that Fred Trump was not intellectual considering how in just a lapse he has gone from the middle class to the elite and privileged one. He is rightly called an intellectual man, someone who has the capacity to create and multiply the United States in work, in building, and in money.

For the full comprehension of each other, being intellectual isn't limited by earning a MASTER's or a PHD from Harvard University, Yale Town.

It's resounding a magnanimous success on his part when we see how his five children including Donald Trump, the fourth shone brightly from all angles to serve their country well. Referring to the background of each of them, we deduce to call it, 5 out of 5 without any fault including Donald Trump, the real architect and master to think.

Among other things, it also noted that any upside-down situation and attitude orchestrated by the Democrats and certain Republicans with an old face and temperament would often favor the Democratic party the most. Sometimes, reflecting on these erroneous and thoughtless anti-Tea Party actions taken by these Republicans in question, in concert with the Democrats, one wonders: how and why do these kinds of face flight? When they know full well that the Democratic party would often be the main beneficiary. It's really ugly to think like that.

However, it remains a real fact given the experience of the current situation pitting Donald Trump vs. Democrats and tough Republicans such as Chris C., M. Romney, Karl R., Barr, and others. Thus, for a serious and correct party like that of the Republican, it should never be like this. However, seeing from a whole Cathedral of red balls on both sides fired at Trump and also without a big obstacle intercepted by the latter, there is no longer any question of getting out of there. It is a certain fact that on both sides, the evil and the harm done to this country is almost incurable.

It is quite lamentable to see that leaders, more specifically Republicans, are not capable of recognizing that the country has been going bad since Biden has taken over. This is a country which is actually in a state of peregrination and peril, reclaiming the full support of each other to get it out of this politic-economic-social pit it has found itself in since the inauguration of President Joe Biden, swearing to repeat for the American people the fabulous Carterian period of 1977-1981 where finding a job was like digging hard to find a piece of silver while the corruptions were everywhere, what plunged the country in a state of inflationary cul-de-sac (dead end), taking a long time for Ronald Reagan to be able to straighten out the situation and bring relief to the unfortunate victims of mismanagement and the Carterian pandemic in all kinds.

If politics is a game of power, why don't Republicans have the courage and even the audacity to take advantage of the bad governance of the Biden administration to score big?

In this concern, if they really are from the country, if they are also Republicans conscious of the nefast effect expecting the country in return, they should let go of all the sentiments of division, hypocrisy, and hatreds to make room for unity in the true sense of the term to save the USA from being under its eternal enemies' banner. To do so, they must not have a short memory to forget great performances of the past with Richard Nixon, 1972, and Ronald Reagan, 1984, ultra-popular everywhere in the United States.

As a result, their incontrovertible popularity allowed them to pulverize their opponent on a score of river by winning forty-nine of the fifty states of the country. These are records that were to be etched in the memory of all conscious Republicans to know that only unity should exist in their midst for the recurrence of such exploits because political leaders without a fixed stability of memory are leaders without a future.

It was not without reason that Ronald Reagan had gained cause even within the Democrat party! Why not follow the same trajectory taken by Ronald Reagan to correct all the disorders of Biden's administration to bring full satisfaction to the Americans and allow them to be confident and stay optimistic. Thus, without intending to talk about Chris Christie, who is already considered as a lost sheep whose political future is buried never to surface again. However, it should be noted that the biggest loser would be Governor DeSantis who, by a miserly ambition, made the greatest political error of his life, that of standing crosswise against the leader who had always defended him tooth and nail (Donald Trump). On this, we deduce that he's also part of the plot orchestrated against Trump.

It is well counted, but miscalculated because being a governor of Florida does not mean you're of the caliber of Ronald Reagan, Richard Nixon, and even Donald Trump who have already been president and proved to the country what they have been doing during their era. As far as DeSantis, you're a Governor who has been backed up by Donald Trump! When was DeSantis so popular to bite the hand that fed him?

Statistics are always there! It's true that Trump has already beaten him up severely before in his own state and before his own people. What about the remaining states, let's not talk about that! It's like an Elephant vs. a skinny goat.

DeSantis must know that Florida is far from being the whole United States of America! This is a fifty-state country! If in your state you're already a victim of Trump's infernal machine, just like Chris, Joe Biden, Hillary, Jeff Bush to name a few, you're done to never resurface.

The song says: "Adieu Lisbonne". On our side, we are content to say: GOODBYE DESANTIS! 2028's DREAM IS COMPLETELY COLLAPSED AND LOST.

Therefore, talking about Ronald Reagan, the letter found an American generation who was very proud of being American and also concerned about the future of the country. Currently, that's quite the contrary that one observes in the

United States. Statistics are really negative when it is a question of patriotism and several other things regarding American culture. The time has changed and people have also changed. However, given how the culture, prestige, and morality often go diminishing, one deduces that it's not good for a better future of this country.

Today, we see ourselves living in an upside-down country where we also see people's lack of attention and respect for the greeting of our national anthem. Sometimes, we're even afraid in some cities of the country to wear the flag, which was supposed to be our pride. All this immorality and lack of patriotism contribute to plunging the country into darkness while our enemies are taking advantage of it to make their own butter.

The problem is the baby fish always follow the trail of the big one. Which amounts to saying that any bad behavior of our politicians has often had repercussions on today's youth. If we, as adults who were to serve as their compass, throw ourselves and soak in all corruption acts and anti-patriotism sentiment, how to ask our young people to act otherwise? In this context, we once again deduce of it to say, the small fish trails the path of the big one! Isn't it?

But what we said before, contrary to Ronald Reagan who did not have to face all these challenges, it was not quite an easy task for Trump. Because whatever he tried to do to improve and prevail, he was prevented from moving an inch with both opponents and numerous people from the same party who discriminated against him. What's worse, it sometimes came from his own so-called collaborators.

The biggest problem again is that the fourth power, which is at 80 percent, has been always anti-Trump and his policy of Americanism in which he puts American people first, more especially the voice of the voiceless.

Thus, to testify of it, let's elaborate on different phases of these recorded obstacles by the administration of Donald Trump.

The question of impeachment regarding Russia-Russia was orchestrated by Hillary and her acolytes, set to be one of the crucial obstacles which was going to slow down the great trajectory of his movement to move forward. Imagine a President freshly elected was already subject to impeachment? There was no way that Trump would be comfortable, while instead of concentrating on his projects of society and the Americanism slogan under which he ran, he was obliged to waste his time by talking to his lawyers and his partisans in both the Senate and Congress to avoid the worst. Therefore, we remained convinced that everything was going well.

The second episode concerned police brutality. People day and nights protested in the streets of several cities of the country. Where was Donald Trump during all these altercations and destructions of our heroes' statues and our public and private institutions? As the commander-in-chief, he had to react as such to assume his responsibility and make sure that the law be applied according to what dictates the Constitution, and he did! There is no reason that people turned the state institution into fire, claiming to defund the police. This is a regrettable incident. We have enough necessary tools in our judiciary systems to investigate, analyze, and render justice where it is due. In this sense, we believe that the best route to follow is allowing our justice to prevail.

President Trump was right when he talked that way because the question of dismantling and defunding the police is not in the Constitution. Anyone with a good sense of reason had to know that President Trump, expressing himself that way, proved once again that he was capable of assuming his responsibility, referring to the principles of law to shed the light for the calm and peace to come back and remain in the country. "No one is above the law," he said then. If the police, no matter what color he is, once found guilty, should be punished according to the law.

However, although assuming his full responsibility in hand to serve the law for an equitable justice, the left still qualified him for racism.

The third chapter of the police defund contrast joined itself to China's Covid-19, in which the question of wearing masks was not a serious preoccupation for the left, who tried to play a brutal game to gain cause. In this context, how to proceed? That of closing all the state, private, and religious institutions because Trump careless about American people's lives. But despite this, yet no formal measure had been taken requiring protestors to wear masks, while at the same time protesting at a distance from each other was supposed to be absolutely imperative!

However, regarding celebrations in the churches, open schools, etc., Donald Trump was the main criminal of his own people who deserved to be crucified, while setting free those considering Barabbas and from whom Covid-19 was spread out.

Nevertheless, to get an idea of how to blame and consider Trump as the main perpetrator was a heinous and filthy crime against the latter. So here is that a proper technician-Doctor belonging to the Wuhan laboratory revealed that the spread of the Virus throughout the world, Covid-19 was not a simple accident. It was well planned and wanted on the part of China that was ultra ambitious and thirsty for the conquest leadership of the world.

Unfortunately, surprised by a Donald Trump all fire, all flames swearing to defeat and proclaim victory by not only preventing China from keeping on treating our farmers as poor patriots, but also demand that the United States recover the majority of our companies which were in China return to the fold for the greatest benefit of the country and the American workers.

In this sense, once thwarted, they had nothing else to do, that of using clever strategies to deviate the good trajectory and the cruising speed of Donald Trump who was to land well and deliver good goods to the American people as was promised. While reproaches were leveled at Trump as the one who invented news and showed terrors by creating division. While also the left had fun firing red balls at Trump and defending China.

Trump's statements were only speculations and erroneous opinions against Beijing. Therefore, currently speaking, the cat is out of the bag. It is a proven fact that Trump was absolutely right. It seemed that Trump was a little mystical, spiritual, not to say prophetic to see further than eyes envisioning China to limit damages of his Covid-19. In contrast to the actual moment where only the United States and China exchanged some two dozen flights a week, in 2019, the number was 365 flights a week between these two countries, about 14 times more than today.

Trump was vigilant enough to understand the game played by China. The statement issued by Trump prohibiting any flight from China was not authorized to land on our airports until further notice was the best. Lamentably, Fauci, in concert with the liberal media, condemned that decision to make it a context of division from Trump's side.

Were not the barriers imposed by Trump's detractors, China's Covid-19 would have caused less damage in terms of the loss of life in the United States because within a week of this announcement accusing Beijing of being the carrier of the virus, Trump was already to curb it by prohibiting any flight from China to land on our runways.

Imagine how it would have been ultra fatal if Trump did not open eyes on Fauci to tell him, no matter what: No fly from China is accepted until further notice; otherwise, instead of 1,133,000 deaths, the number should have been triple in the United States. But in all of this was just the beginning of the hurdles encountered by Trump on China's Covid-19. However, it is the most difficult of all means to find a vaccine as quickly as possible to slow the spread of this pandemic.

Thus, awaiting the curable vaccine, it has been revealed that traditional medicine using tea made up of a leaf called MUGWORT had already alleviated a lot of suffering patients. Knowing that it's not a road that leads to Rome, the brave Donald Trump made it his duty to tell people that if they drink in this area and they feel relief, that they continue to do so if they want to. Thus, the President was crystal clear above. Therefore, it was not a surprise to see the leftist media use it once again to call President Trump a criminal opting for the death of the American people.

Despite all these bitter critics, the President was still right because a lot of foreigners followed this method and survived before the vaccine was available, especially senior citizens like me.

What people of comprehension and common sense like about Donald Trump is that he's always optimistic. He never gets tired. He always keeps his calm to live with hope that tomorrow will be even more beautiful, what a leader applying to lead a country like ours must refer to in order to deliver well to people.

As a result, despite China, Covid-19 is almost over; many people still use mugwort, garlic, lemon, ginger, and cloves to keep their immune system strong against a possible return of this pandemic, China's Covid-19! Who knows?

As for me, in my sixties, I still use both, Trump's Pfizer and this traditional medicine in question. Why not?

Anyway, thank you, Mister President, for such wonderful advice. The proof was so great, in a corrupt and unhealthy place like Haiti, China Covid-19 was not vulnerable! The few vaccines sent there were sold and used by the bourgeois class. Therefore, the unfortunates had no access to Pfizer. Once again, thanks to the traditional medicine mentioned above because Haiti is one of the few countries where the pandemic wreaked havoc. About 860 deaths out of 12 million people living in this country.

Meanwhile, referring to the suffering endured by Jesus before his death on the cross, we would have a tendency to liken such suffering to that of Trump during that crucial period. Wanting to act as quickly as possible to bring the pandemic under control before it was too late, President Trump has fulfilled Fauci's role as the main responsible in this field.

This is how we found Donald Trump super determined to maintain close and tight contacts with several laboratory companies such as Moderna, Pfizer, and many others to find in a record time a miraculous vaccine and get the country out of this pandemic crisis called the Chinese malediction. But unfortunately, the anti-change forces had not hesitated even for a second to sacrifice Trump to make people understand that if Trump is going to present us with a vaccine between six and 11 months, it is something bad that will cause more harm than good to the health of the American people. Scientists are unanimous in recognizing that it was only in 1960 that a vaccine was found so quickly.

Despite everything, it was within the interval of four years. In this sense, Trump was said to be a dreamer, an exaggerator. In other words, it is a mission impossible, said his detractors.

Finally, the record of 1960 has been greatly beaten, more than four times by Trump because the United States of America found the vaccine as it has been announced. On December 14, 2020, vaccinations in the United States began. Promises made, promises kept. i.e., (January 20, 2020 - December 14, 2020).

Although, a lot of people, especially senior citizens whose brains have been washed by the media were still reticent for the first dose. When asked where does this fear come from when the President of the country, Donald J. Trump, was one of the first people to be vaccinated? On this point, it is necessary to repeat after the other when he said; People who do not have a good memory to remember good things are people without a future. What they don't figure out is that the United States means a gift from beyond.

No doubt, it is not without reason that the emblem of our currency formulates such a wonderful and meaningful thought: IN GOD WE TRUST. It's not something that has just come out of the mouth. It is an inspiring and spiritual thought that holds all its importance and value in our way of thinking and acting to achieve serious things and live well. Whether we like it or not, Donald Trump is the leader we need in 2024 to safeguard such an achievement from beyond.

This is a golden and diamond opportunity with Trumpets and others for a full landing this time around. Take advantage of it because time lost can never be made up.

NEVER FORGET. ALWAYS REMEMBER IT.

The passage of China's COVID-19 must remain incarcerated in our memory as the worst experience of the 21st century. This date of January 20, 2020, must serve as an example for us to never give a mandate to anyone with an ultra-liberal and patri-pocket in connivance with our notary enemies to lead the country. Thus, we don't believe your memory is already short to not be able to see and understand what is currently happening in the USA with so-called anti-racist and discrimination leaders having become super miserly to sell our country dirt cheap, not to say at a ridiculous price.

That's why, the Architect and leader of the Americanism ideology begs you with a certain insistence to swear that such shenanigans will not be repeated under the banner of your Americanophile, Donald Trump, whose only objective will be quickly moving forward to M-A-G-A in 2024.

Remember once again, my dear compatriots: A people without memory is a people without a future. Also, remember that our roots are profound and numerous. Whether they like it or not, we shall prevail for the greatest benefit of this country, especially for those forgotten men and women.

This is a way to say that we will not forget January 20,

2020, and that drastic measures must be taken to not come back to always the same. But there again, although he began a struggle to encourage Americans to get more vaccines, Trump was going to face an oligarchy of major Republican donors and Democratic backers, staunch Obama-Biden-Hillary supporters.

Those Republicans in question wanted to impose on him their own traditional agenda, which has nothing to do with that of Donald Trump. As a result, the latter refuted them all, preferring to fight alongside the American people in his agenda of Americanism. Trump let them know that even when it is often said that the main is metamorphic, as far as I'm concerned, I will never change my mind. I must keep a promise made to the voiceless.

That fierce fight between them and Donald Trump does not date from today. It already dated from 2016 during the debate for the primaries where Trump was to demean the Bush family, General Colin Powell, more precisely Governor Jeb Bush, with whom he was measuring himself for the Republican party nomination and meet with Hillary Clinton in the general election on November 8, 2016. Thus, as indicated above, Trump did not put water in his mouth to fire big red balls at the Bush family for this useless war in Iraq, which caused considerable damages in human lives and in economic means. Criticizing someone is not as quite painful and fatal as one might think. However, it depends on who is criticizing. Someone of Trump's caliber, of a loudspeaker voice, especially when he finds out that his opponent is guilty, the way he proceeds to erase you on the political scene remains a major asset of which he alone holds the secret. It is in this sense that Trump was able to refresh the memory of the American people to win his case through the Republican primaries, but also against Hillary Clinton, whom he had also beaten by a river score, electorally speaking.

OLIGARCHY AND GLOBALIZATION SECRET

The reason why there always exists conflicts between superpower countries and those of the third ones is a question of interest. It does not often happen unexpectedly. Contrary to China or Russia, where Putin or Xi have the power to do as they wish, the United States, as a democratic country, does not allow the President of the country to behave as master and lord. It is quite a flagrant violation of the republican and democratic principle for a President to hold the full power to act and govern as he pleases.

In this context, not having this right is an imperative to create other opportunities to find a way to get rich, just like Vladimir Putin and so many other leaders of Communist and Arab countries. This is called interest conflict, which has all its reason to exist.

Without going back further, Iraq, Afghanistan, Libya, and Haiti, to name a few, the situation in Ukraine is good enough to have an idea of the reality of the facts. But to really act as master and lord, your party must be in power. What's essential that gives you full authority to nominate and revoke is when you have the full control of the Congress and Senate. For instance, being a full power Secretary of State under Obama's leadership, Hillary Clinton did not hesitate to elect a stupid cracker who was terminated in fifth place in the primary election in 2011 in Haiti, while the two first candidates supposed to go to the second tour for none of them reaching 50+1 during the first round. As a result, all fire, all flames, Hillary ordered her subaltern to force the President of the country to eliminate one of the two first place candidates to allow the stupid cracker to be elected President in 2011. There again, according to the Director in Chief and responsible of the electoral counsel to publish the results of the elections, he said, "It was not the result published in the Journal of the Monitor, I did publish!"

Embarrassed by several interrogations from journalists of different media, the Responsible Director answered, "My duty was to realize these elections and publish the result. So, the government in concert with the high external hierarchy has judged it necessary to do otherwise, what do you want me to do more?"

Moreover, he said, as a provisional director of the electoral council, the elections once finished, my work was also finished. It was in this sense, we heard the President then say in a short interview, "If you want to assassinate me or put me in jail, you can still do so. But the world will be able to judge you for your actions." It's at that time we knew that the weakness of the president in question came from the big pressure of Hillary and her minions to send a crystal clear message to the latter, namely, "THE AIRPLANE WAS ALREADY AT THE AIRPORT WAITING FOR YOU TO DECIDE AND GIVE YOUR FINAL WORD."

Moreover, the Director of the electoral office added that the candidate really elected had to give up not only because she was a woman like a ship surrounded by wild national and international lions but also a sexagenarian intellectual feared for her life.

WHAT ABOUT CURRENTLY SPEAKING?

Everybody is living what is going on in Ukraine. When Trump tried to apply his policy of anti-corruption, knowing that Ukraine was one of the countries obtaining a PhD in matters of corruption of all kinds, asked the president-elect to be careful because under my administration, the United States is not going to support any country involved in corruption. In everybody's eyes, it was a legitimate statement issued by President Trump whose objective was to protect the interest of the American people. Unfortunately, with a super trio composed by Schiff, Pelosi, and Schumer to only name these three, Donald Trump was the pet peeve who deserved to go to hell because he tried to intimidate his opponent.

This is a brutal and fatal violation of the principle of our democracy. And what are we actually living? What a dirty situation to see our country has been mortgaged by so many anti-patriot democrats, not to say patri-pockets. For more than 7 years, those placed in the headquarters of the government managed to sell the country at a low price! What happens to the land of Washington, Abraham Lincoln?

There is no reason not to like Donald Trump and RFK Jr., who are camped in crossfire to thwart these kinds of such dirty behavior, plunging our country into a mess of a dead-end situation not to resurface.

Therefore, given the strength that this globalism has taken during Biden's administration, to repeat Mark Levin, if it can't be stopped now, it should be too late in the distant future. This system is so strong and ruthless that only the strongest will be saved, not the most innocent and just because the recent testimony of Dr. Gal Luft, an ocular witness at the helm of Ukraine-Biden shenanigans, is enough to explain everything on this subject. Unfortunately, innocent that he is, Dr. Gal Luft, thinking that he was doing a favor to a country which is not even his, denouncing the shenanigans between Biden and the Ukraine team, he was fatally sold by ensnaring the oligarchs as the vanguard force of Ucrano-USA whose Biden and Hunters are the so-called big and small guys.

That was well thought, but miscalculated by the poor and miserable Doctor who knows how to run, but not how to hide to be very sumptuous and let himself be caught in the trap set for him by the heads of the high hierarchic supporters of the globalism system.

The examples of these kinds of situations are so numerous and often repeated that we would need a lot of time and whistleblowers for a long gossip, which is not considered a small task. Can so many others living on the run like Dr. Gal be brave enough to accept to put himself at the disposal of Congress to testify and tell the truth? It would not be easy to find several others of his caliber to risk their life and family's to do the same for the comprehension of the public to shed light.

Therefore, as far as this important witness pitting Congress vs. Biden-Hunter, China, Ukraine, and Romania, Dr. Gal looks also like a car running on a muddy slope including a cliff to the right and to the left. He's already in a situation of dead end where any move he makes will cost him a heavy price to pay.

In consequence, being ready to testify on this affair would do more good than harm because he considers himself a dead man on vacation who has nothing to lose, but everything to gain. It is resignation that makes the man. Stay on the run, I'm not safe. It is better attending Congress; at least like that, my disappearance, once programmed, would be at least public in the eyes of everyone to know what is happening. But the question that more than one might ask, will this Congress be capable of making him come out from the run to testify? Does it exist willing to do so? Would these oligarchs hierarchically give the green light to make it happen?

Anyway, questions which are still pending to which it remains perplexed to have a positive response.

By the way, all these upside-down situations of the shenanigans regarding indictment and others are taking place because of these coming elections. It's a very important step for them to make their butter. It's an excellent opportunity which is not supposed to be missed because it's towards this period of these elections that must be well planned in order to give the country the color of their choice. Therefore, to everything there is time.

The question that everyone does not hesitate to ask: will 2024 be the same as 2020? In that year, a lot of controversies have occurred with China's COVID-19, protests almost everywhere including impeachment and several partisans of George W. Bush, Colin Powell, Dick Cheney to only name a few who were crossfire against Donald Trump.

However, taking consciousness of how the country is going bad, perhaps they would have already changed their mind to see they are also responsible for having boycotted Trump and give green light to Biden in 2020!

According to a mediatic source that we can trust, despite the winds and tides of the leaders of the oligarchic school, the people would have the chance this time to elect the best president of their choice. One of the problems which was confronted, was the independence for some reason that the reason itself seems ignored until now. However, being the main victims of the bad inflationary policy of Biden, they are fed up and opt to shun the latter's candidacy to make their choice towards another candidate whose Trump has a big chance to benefit from it to fill the void.

After all that occurred in Arizona, Georgia, and Pennsylvania respectively in 2020 and 2022, especially in Arizona, these concerned instances are going to do their best to give to Caesar what belongs to him. In other words, on November 5, 2024, the best candidate will be the winner because we can't tolerate seeing countries like the Dominican Republic, Brazil to only name those two to organize elections and that the same day, the results are already known while the number one country on earth, with all our capacity and technology as being a true brain seller country, can't do it, even faster! All the tools are right there to do it well. Unfortunately, is it always oligarchic hierarchical fervent and addictive supporters of the globalistic system always to camp on the cross to reverse the process and make it obsolete, which processes that of M-A-G-A.

However, what makes our country look ugly. Anyway,

American people must know that only a handful of elites should never decide for them. They must be able to know that allowing such interference and tolerance will always mean a victory in apotheosis for the oligarchs but a long suffering for the hard class workers in the future because they have been going through it for the last three years and it is revealed to be painful according to the latter. In this context, they must be able to set an example in 2024 to avoid the repetition and continuation of such electoral shenanigans of which, themselves as working people and middle class are and will always be the main losers.

Also, if memory does not fail you, we would be very pleased for your archive and your understanding to brush a little bit the dark board and the indecisive days that these swing states like Michigan, Wisconsin, and very precisely Pennsylvania, especially the latter which was really in a state of electoral crisis where a lot of frauds, violations of electoral laws, and so many others were claimed by the Republicans, more especially Trump's campaign.

If the two first swing states mentioned above were already decided, as far as Pennsylvania, it was the permanence in all its forms which was declared for over two weeks. For this reason, Trump's supporters claimed a penalty against Biden for flagrant election frauds.

After winning big in Ohio, Florida, while leading in Michigan and Wisconsin by 1.30% where 83% of the votes were already counted, Trump only needed to carry both Wisconsin and Michigan or only Pennsylvania to reach 270 electorates and win the 2020 presidential election.

If these two previous, namely Michigan and Wisconsin, were at risk, as for Pennsylvania, in the eyes of everyone, that was a game almost over because at midnight on November 3, after 75% of counting of the votes, President Donald Trump was up by 11% over Biden whether by 700,000 votes with only 25% remaining to be counted. What was quite ultra false! We can prove it by simple elementary math! 75% of a total (6,936,803 × 75% = 5,202,602 votes) of which Trump was up with 700,000. If Trump was up by this 700,000 in question, that 75% of the count gave him 3,301,301 votes while Biden had 1,901,301 votes! But instead of 11% up, it should have been 27%.

So, with only 25% votes remaining, you want to tell us that Biden not only made up the deficit of 700,000 votes but also won by 80,555 votes. But again, there is nuance. We must not forget according to FOX-NEWS, there is a remaining 25% of votes evaluating at 1,400,000 left. Therefore, in reference to Google, this 25%, contrary to Fox-News representing 1,634,201 votes remained to be counted.

Despite everything, it would seem that either one or the other is wrong because if it was 1,400,000 votes we were shown to have Biden win by 80,555 votes more than Trump! So from this data, we could say: 700,000 + 80,555 = 780,555 votes for Biden + 1,901,301 = 2,681,856 votes, which is not accurate when we know that Biden totalized 3,459,923 votes. Actually, let's get away from FOX's to focus on Google on this question of this 25% remaining which is 1,734,201 votes. So, in order for Biden to obtain 3,459,923 votes, he has to win from the remaining 25%, a total of 1,558,622 votes + 1,901,301 = 3,459,923. As far as Trump, it would be 1,734,201 - 1,558,622 = 175,579 votes for Donald Trump, which represent only 9% of votes from 1,734,201.

Wow! It is often said that the impossible is not English! However, to almost everyone, if the word impossible doesn't exist, it will be necessary to invent it to say: IT'S IMPOSSIBLE!

It was not without reason that after midnight of that time, sitting in the East room of the White House, Trump, noting that only a miracle could prevent him from winning the state of Pennsylvania, arrogated to himself the right to proclaim himself victorious in this key said state. Therefore, an announcement that in the first place aroused the anger of this rodent fox on the FOX NEWS OF COURSE!, supposedly Donald Trump's renowned adviser, Chris Christie. Unfortunately, it was that same caressing hypocrite with the fox's face who was the first one to find President Trump exaggerated, abnormal, and even overwhelmed by events.

Taking the risk towards his intervention on FOX's prematurely declaring himself the winner in the State of Pennsylvania was quite an irresponsible action. It was not a secret that he consistently knew there were still 25% of votes left to be counted.

But what Chris doesn't want to understand is that Donald Trump is not an ordinary person as Chris would have a tendency to believe. Donald Trump is spiritual, mystic, and prophetic. It's not without reason that one would constantly compare him to JESUS. But you would say that is ugly to compare a spiritual man to a sinner! But the bible says, God made man in his image. Provided one acts in righteousness, you will be able by divine power to accomplish anything you want for your people and your country. It is in this sense that we see in Trump a man guided by the beyond to be born again in order to accomplish this mission, that of, MAKE AMERICA GREAT AGAIN.

DON'T WE SEE THIS BIT OF SIMILARITY BETWEEN THOSE TWO THROUGH THE ENDURED SUFFERING ON THE JOURNEY OF DOING GOOD?

We must note again we are living on a big piece of land called the United States of America, a sacred land guided by the Universe. For this particular reason, no matter what shenanigans are orchestrated by the dark forces, Trump will reverse all obstacles and prevail. It is not quite a Trump affair! This is what the master of the universe wants! Can't we see despite every invented bad reports about Trump, his popularity goes increasing while that of his multiple opponents including Biden, tremendously goes diminishing?

Therefore, Trump's pilgrimage and his final success in 2024 will serve as a good moral and political lesson which will prove once again that man has the right to propose, but GOD IS THE ONE TO DISPOSE.

Not wanting you to act in Saint Thomas—you only believe when you see—he has already set before you all a series of signs announcing what might happen if you keep trying to thwart his vision towards a good life system for the people of this country. He's about to allow you to see with your own eyes all of the abominations regarding transgenders, of men and women abolishing the law of God, throwing it away in the basket. The interference of our enemies in our country and so many dirty behaviors. So, when this deaf ear and blindfold will reach such an exaggerated level, and that, although seeing it crystal clear before you, you still care less, at this point will come the real heaven's wrath.

Meanwhile, Donald Trump might not be able to do anything right away because the universe would give you some real moments of suffering, allowing you to learn your lessons well before Trump can bring relief.

Trump will not be too much affected because he did what he has been told to do! You are the ones who were in absolute rebellion, not to listen. What we must know is that he worked hard to become wealthy, while the other did so at the expense of the sweat of your front and your courage, not only for his own profit but also for that of his overseas partners.

What we're living actually appears to be the beginning. Without a magic wand in hands to foresee things, but it is your Friday which will tell you how your Saturday will look like. The reason why our enemies would be able to take over it's because we should be out of cash. It's not without reason that China, in concert with other partners, was the first country to opt for a devaluation and collapse of the American's currency. When that happens, our dollar would no longer be universal.

It's not a small task, the war in Ukraine. China is a good partner of Russia. According to several sources, despite this infernal war with Ukraine, Russia's economy is not as vulnerable as the United States. No one needs to be an expert in this domain to know it.

We never stop borrowing one billion dollars from Japan and China every day. Instead of producing oil and gas, we purchase them from overseas, such as Venezuela actually. The same China from which we borrow seizes the opportunity on our border crisis to invade our country with illicit products subject to destroying our rising youth, calling for succession. As a country called: brain's sellers, if it happens that we are no longer able to produce well-rounded and well-made brains, we'll be completely out of business. What we others would not ever wish for our country, while the great clerks who are at the helm of businesses are not of the same opinion. In this sense, more than one would ask: what to do, since the reason of the greatest is always the best?

Therefore, being trapped by all kinds of vicious circles, we would ask perplexed if only one social would be able to reverse the situation? There is still a glimmer of hope to heal this wound. That claims that the people become aware of the seriousness and dangerous turn of the crisis. The latter must know that they have a responsibility to make their voice heard to avoid any unnecessary consequence since they will be the very first to be victims. But there again, there is a problem because deprived of everything in this difficult period, it could well be these people let themselves be bought by the oligarchs. This could easily happen when you consider how even those who are smart and wealthy become voracious to sell the country at ridiculous prices. What about those who are poor?

Anyway, given that it is no longer the oligarchs' globalists who will decide. The people suffering, despite this, could hold the sword to the end. Let's hope so!

Thus, as we have just noted above, nobody will know what will happen in 2024 for everything to be easy-going and that all the streets will be peacefully celebrating the victory in the apotheosis of Donald Trump.

To contrary to 2016, it will be joy everywhere in the United States. That's the way the guy upstairs will decide it. Then if Barack Obama could, why not also the Master of the Universe? The sign of peace will take place by awareness that it is on the Republican side as well as on that of Democrats, even the most liberal and zealous because their personal interest will also be in danger! They too, will be able to understand that the United States is currently seen as a country already mortgaged at a ridiculous price to another superpower, not to say: China and that for this particular reason, this demands obligatorily that something must totally change in this country. And it is from this change of government and policy that we will see Donald J. Trump managed to present and detail before the nation the full content of his philosophy of Americanism to MAKE AMERICA GREAT AGAIN.

Many people already think that once elected, Donald Trump will be all fire all flames to become resentful, vengeful, and voracious to take in sandwich and make a double bite with his political opponents, including the enemies from overseas. But it would be wrong to think so because you will see a Donald Trump deliver his victory speech, but the sermon to deliver will come somewhere else. Whether the left like it or not, they must agree with him. You imagine Donald Trump after a month of governance, drilling in Texas and Alaska, downs the price of fuel is down to 2.50 the gallon instead of 3.50 it is currently sold! What the left will be able to do about it? Give a chance this time to the Americanism of Donald Trump to make its great merry way towards progress; otherwise, your listening will be affected. So, people aren't watching and listening to TV and Radio, you won't be able to continue operating. As a result, is to leave aside all the past bitter critics to make room for peace and union because that is the only Union that makes us a real force to redeem us from the hand of the enemy.

It is often said that the past is the past; let's think of now and the future. Nevertheless, it should be noted that these three times work together. There is a time to know how to say: it's already gone, let's forget it! But it's not always the case, especially with regard to the 2020 presidential elections in the United States. Because it's from this past error that we are going to lead ourselves to make big corrections in 2024, by saying that similar regrettable incidents of this kind must not repeat.

How did these electoral incidents happen in 2020? As noted above, after having well swept the three important swing states, North Carolina, Ohio, and Florida, Donald Trump, with the big wind in his sails, was the only rooster to crow in the barnyard, ready to win the elections. He needed to win one or two of the three states, either Pennsylvania or Michigan-Wisconsin, to collapse Sleepy Joe and collect these 270+1 electorates. By the way, it was about midnight in Pennsylvania when 75% of the votes were already counted while Donald Trump led big over Sleepy Joe, with an 11% advantage on the scoreboard, i.e., 700,000 votes.

As far as Wisconsin and Michigan, a whopping 1.83% in advance while 83% of the votes were already cast. Even when there were doubts about these two last states, especially since Trump's superiority was a little minimal. However, regarding Pennsylvania, no one thought Sleepy Joe could not only wake up but also resurface to finally win this state of Pennsylvania by a whopping 80,555 votes. "Wow!" exclaimed MAGA's supporter. "Penalty, Referee! Handball! No good! It doesn't count!" Thus, these referees replied; it's already in the nets, the goal is validated!

How did they manage to proclaim victory? What able tactics did they use to win the state of Pennsylvania? Contrary to Mister Bill Gates, who, without a fraction of a second, bitterly criticized Trump for being too premature on Fox News, proclaiming himself the winner of the State of Pennsylvania. Regarding several other people, Chris is the one who was wrong when, in the eyes of everyone, they stopped counting the 25% remaining of the ballots to reschedule for the next 7 days, we had to know some shenanigans were about to take part in this process.

To testify its veracity, a simple accounting language, 'FIFO' through which, just like they did it for Wisconsin and Michigan: First ballot received, first ballot counted. Instead, the opposite had happened because mailing ballots, which, especially from local couriers, were supposed to be counted first when we know they were received earlier for the most part. Moreover, a little elementary math level can easily shed light.

In Philly, for example, a bastion of the Democrats and

black voters, about 705,000 people cast their vote of which 81% were Democrats while 18% were Republicans. But more than 75% of these were already counted before the counting process was stopped. We have seen, read, and analyzed all the data and statistics showing that Biden has broken the voting record in Pennsylvania and even surpassed the first black President, Barack Obama, everywhere in that regard.

Therefore, despite all, something had appeared fishy and doubtful. Why did they stop counting after midnight? Such was, at first, the question that more than one asks in this concern.

Were they right thinking that way? Far from being a judge to pronounce the verdict to whom deserving it, a question of good sense would allow us to understand that such a counting process is not a daily duty where workers, feeling tired, must take a break in order to have more energy for the following days because it's a permanent job. What is quite contrary to an election process taking place every four years.

We can also understand, if it was a matter of technique where these machines were not capable of achieving the process, that pretext should have been excusable and acceptable. And there again, there was nuance because technicians had to be present to expect all these kinds of problems to finally solve them at close range. In this sense, they would have allowed the counting process to make its way for a reliable, adequate, and correct work finish.

Presidential elections in the United States are not a small task. We are talking about the most important historic event in the number one country on earth! We are the compass for other countries in this area for the triumph of democracy throughout the world! But as the main leader, if we violate these democratic norms and achievements, how can we ask those fierce dictators of the other countries in question to bring corrections to their democratic notebooks? It was not a surprise to hear them say after the 2020 elections, especially in the States of Pennsylvania, the United States must be the first one to make the first step before asking other countries to do the same. In other words, to repeat after the other, the United States must clean the windows of their houses first before telling neighbors that theirs are dirty.

As mentioned above, analyses and statistics of all kinds tried to speculate to explain and certify the last-minute defeat of Donald Trump in Pennsylvania. However, there is never smoke without fire. Besides, if I know I can beat an opponent, how to create controversies to adjourn the counting of the remaining 25% processes for seven more days, causing Republican voters to camp en masse in front of the tabulation center in protest?

According to what formulates the electoral law, both Republicans and Democrats sent as observers have the right to follow the counting processes. However, the opposite occurred after this premature closing of the Philly center of tabulation. As a result, on Wednesday and Thursday, those Republican observers were kicked out and were not allowed to re-enter, just like Democrats, to observe that process. As a reference, the testimony of two of them on Fox News, November 5, 2020, thus, for your full comprehension on this matter, it's not quite difficult to figure it out and shed light for more than 6,936,000 million voters of the said state, Pennsylvania.

At midnight on November 5, 2020, after the counting of 75% of the votes, which is 5,202,602 (five million, two hundred thousand, and six hundred two), Donald Trump was highly up by seven hundred thousand votes over Biden (700,000).

Without wanting to go through the four paths to certify it, this process seemed to have been backward since after midnight on November 5, 2020. Let's detail this process to allow us to see a little clearer.

We can understand that in the state of Pennsylvania, the Democrats registered to vote are in the majority. Although, did they really choose to vote that way in 2020? But also, statistics revealed that the margin would have gone diminishing lately for more Democrats changing party than vice versa. Anyway, leading by 700,000 votes after 75% of counting while only 25% remaining, about 1,400,000 votes, Trump couldn't realize at least 351,000, which is 26%?

So even 351,000 was an impossible mission for Trump? According to our little math, from these remaining ballots, we can see that Trump was fraudulently pulverized by Joe Biden, so-called the super and ultra-democratic popular candidate in 2020! Wow, we didn't know that!

On this point, we would like to refer you to a Banana Republic where a provisional president after a coup had the chance to become a provisional president.

This President in question was considered as a moron, novice, and dwarf, in politics by supporters because he wanted to sit down with his main opponents to have an agreement on a "D" date for the organization of the general election in the country in question.

He responded to all who are against his decision: “as not only a Republican in principle with a democratic belief, I have a duty and responsibility to invite them to my square, but also because I could easily beat them all, my three opponents. So if I could beat them all in this electoral process, why do shenanigans to create more conflicts in the country? So it is in this sense that we say, why such an adjournment of the counting until the next day? Why also this count is quite partisan in a closed circuit blocking the presence of the Republican observers as required by electoral law in matters of counting? So just as the anecdote related above, if Biden's supporters were so optimistic believing that he could win Pennsylvania, why not have acted as Democrats in principle?”

In summary, Trump, who was leading on the scoreboard by 700,000 after the counting of 75% of the votes, evaluating a total of five million two hundred thousand two and six hundred two votes (5,202,602), finally had to lower his victory flag to be fraudulently beaten worse than Kari Lake in Arizona during the 2022 Senatorial race.

As a result, Joe Biden obtained more than 90% of the remaining votes, about one million five hundred fifty-eight thousand six hundred twenty-two ballots while Trump did less than 10%. Many people, especially Republican voters, found it unbelievable, not to say very ugly, because not only Joe Biden, who was very profound underwater at midnight on November 4, resurfaced to fill a deficit of 700,000 votes, but also surpassed President Trump by 80,555 according to the board in charge to finally win the state of Pennsylvania just like a Delano Roosevelt and Ronald Reagan-like feat or performance concretized by President Joe Biden in the swing state of Pennsylvania in 2020.

Therefore, as said above, millions of Trumpets still cannot forget, considering it as a shameful glory because to conquer without peril, said the great French writer of the 17th century, Pierre Corneille, we triumph without honor because in politics, an inglorious victory is almost always temporary and doomed to failure, which we are undoubtedly currently experiencing with Biden in power whose policy of sloppiness is about to destabilize so badly, that even his own supporters, zealous Democrats, would have a tendency to compare him worse than a Jimmy Carter from 1980.

Fortunately, several Democrats realized that Biden is no longer up to the task and decided to drop him, opting for the choice of another Democratic candidate. But there again, the Democratic school surrounded and placed under the supervision of the super five dangers: Obama, Joe, Kamala, Schumer, and Schiff, have served the party so much as their wooden horse, that all others following them are also like Chris Christie in bad shape, not to say very behind the rear seat of the bus for 2024.

The question that more than one would want to ask, given how Trump is flying like an eagle towards destiny, is: do they have a potential candidate to take over from Biden to thwart a Donald Trump currently all fire, all flames?

First of all, Kamala is considered worse than Dan Quayle of George H. W. Bush. Will they choose the Senator from California? Oh, no! Two of the super five replied, "Are you crazy? Do you want this said senator to transform the remaining 49 states into homeless areas?" What about Robert F. Kennedy Jr. (RFK Jr.)? No, and no again, unanimously replied the team of super five in question because not only did RFK Jr. bitterly criticize the party for having flagrantly violated the true concept and ideology of his uncle and father, leaving aside all the good things on which the party was built for an American solid and respected.

Secondly, they found him having a brace of similarity with Trump through certain political ideology, which they really don't want to hear and digest. Finally, RFK Jr. appeared to be someone they can't dictate to do this, to do that.

As a result, we can see that on both sides regarding the Democrats, the evil would seem to be already badly over in 2023-2024. As far as Pennsylvania, many Democrats are frustrated for having elected an incompetent and sick senator who represents them in Washington. The other day, being in a restaurant in Philly, we observed two fellow Democrats watching Senator Ted Cruz and Hawley asking tough questions to, respectively, the FBI director and the General Attorney; they were upset because they are super and ultra liberal left-wing Democrats. We heard them say: "What about Fetterman? Why does he never talk?"

Meanwhile, the MAGA has continued to run very fast to make its merry way. In this context, Trumpets have already begun exclamation: "Let Biden's moribund system die!" It appears that Trump's era for 2023-2024 is already announced under the colors of red to become a real phenomenon because it is all the Media for the most, Youtube, Instagram, TikTok, Facebook to only name a few, revealing that the name of Donald Trump is the most quoted in the world.

According to a source of which I remain anonymous, Donald Trump's name is mentioned more than 10,000 times a day throughout the world, including 6,000 times in the United States itself. But that source did not make allusion or mention of his popularity or anything else.

As far as the United States, the black media has been doing an excellent job by educating their fellow brothers to avoid being manipulated every four years by special black multimillionaires to talk about discrimination and racism in America for their own profit in order to continue to do their best to their detriment and naivety.

These black programs, well watched and listened to, don't hesitate to defend Donald Trump from head to toe against the labels of the question of racism and discrimination that those oligarchs of all kinds have always tried to stick on his back.

Nevertheless, what attracts the most is the attention of those fervent Trump's black defenders seeing despite all the criticism lamented against him on racism and discrimination, he had never revealed how he used to help black leaders such as Reverend Jesse Jackson and little Reverend Al, to only enumerate those two, whom he always welcomed with open arms when it's matter to the cause of the black community.

Meanwhile, even one day, we had never heard him in his own voice talking about those favors rendered to the black community because he always said when it comes to help the country, it is no longer a question of white or black. It is preferably a question of helping American people. Meanwhile, on the side, that is to say, left radical traditional media, such as CNN, ABC, and more specifically MSNBC with a Rachel who has always tried to scare people with a lot of lies regarding Donald Trump. She lets the 24 thousand people watching her TV show know that their democratic freedom will be in danger because his congress will put a snout in the mouth of anyone who disagrees with him.

From this moment, as mentioned above, we can see that these types of journalists of the caliber of Rachel turn out to be the real raptors who work tirelessly to accomplish the diabolical mission entrusted to them, that of continuing to destabilize Donald Trump and bring him down forever. However, what those radical left media didn't realize until now is that the storm is over.

They have become quite foolish to not pay any attention. They don't even have the decency to at least refer themselves to the source of history to meditate on all that has been already said. They have preferably passed their entire youth, adult, and old age to preach and hallucinate the lies, inducing in error those who listen to them. They have also become deaf and blindfolded to continue to swim profoundly into the dirt of the negativity interpellation of satanic spirits to convince innocent and naive listeners. That's the way those devils function. That's the way it has always been and still is, that of ignoring the fact to prefer lies. In this context, we must allude to Jesus because despite all these accomplished miracles, those sacrifices still ignored the latter was not of their caliber. He's special, spiritual, invisible, and invincible.

Just like Trump, they don't figure out that since 2016, without being tired, they have persecuted this guy until the current moment. But despite all those upside-down critics, Donald has become more popular. But then, if the Jews did not want to know who Jesus was, how could fervent believers in sin like the Morning Joe Show and Rachel's one be asked to leave Donald Trump alone or give him a break!

Thus, Trump, as a good searcher, goes back to the 18th century to find the great French comedian, Philippe Nericault, to resurface his thoughts in front of his eternal detractors, namely: Criticism is always easy, but Art remains very difficult. That said, it is easier for people to criticize Donald Trump, but ultra-difficult for them to realize what he has already achieved. In this context, Trump's message is crystal clear to them, namely: The dog can still keep barking; he has plenty of right to do so. However, not to forget that Trump's caravan continues to speed by to MAKE AMERICA GREAT AGAIN.

SOLUTION FOR AN IMMIGRATION REFORM

It's no secret when it comes to reliable immigration reform, Republicans are always in the spotlight. In this regard, we would like to refer to Ronald Reagan. Also, as the nation's attention turns back to the fractured debate over an upside-down immigration system after the Carter era, it might be helpful and necessary for the good memory and comprehension of one another to remember that in 1986 testified a great date, not to say a memorable one where Ronald Reagan signed a sweeping immigration reform bill into law. It was not perfect.

However, it allowed almost three million people entering this country illegally before 1982 to benefit from it. It was not a surprise that several Democrats, as always, conceived it as a failure. On this point, Philippe Nericault was right when he said: Criticism is easier, but art remains very difficult. Reagan couldn't satisfy everybody, but at least 3 million people are not either 300 or 3000 thousand people compared to Biden's demagogy currently speaking. This is the day vs. the night.

So many Americans don't pay attention, but that is the worst immigration invasion that this country has ever known. Sometimes, we would ask ourselves, is it because Biden is 81 years old and that he has nothing to lose but everything to gain? What makes him arrogate to himself the right to act fiercely out of wickedness against the people who put him in power? Was he really elected by these people in question? According to the immigration law, President Biden acting that way is a flagrant violation because the President does not have the authority to go it alone in this area. Though in majority, Biden was to work in concert with both chambers for mutual consent instead of practicing his leaving-behind policy for the illegal entry of million immigrants of all feathers onto United States soil with all the risks of danger that might come.

There is what is called, deceptive appearance. It is this cover that Democrats always wrap and camouflage themselves in order to bluff people into believing that they are the only ones on their side.

It is very unfortunate that many Americans have so far failed to discover all the meaning behind these deceptive appearances by Democratic leaders. Exposing and expressing such a flattering tactic from the Democrats is just to go back to 2001 where President George W. Bush proposed an amnesty law to legalize the status of all illegal aliens including benefits and restrictions that would have come with it. Unfortunately, despite his majority in both chambers, that proposition of law has been refuted by these caressing hypocrites, fervent supporters of the poor because not only it was not advantageous for them, but also if such a proposition would have become law, George W. Bush was going to be more popular because it would bring a lot of lost income to this country.

In this perspective, we deduce that as long as the American people don't open their eyes to stop accepting the night for the day, the country will always be subject to collapse and that the great Chinese ambition will see its dream become reality, that of being master and Lord of the world.

Therefore, placed under Divine protection, Donald Trump, despite winds and tides, will not go anywhere you might think. He will survive and still be alive so that once sworn in on January 20, 2025, he will correct all Biden's shenanigans in state affairs to apply a system of migration beneficial to the United States where the law will be applied and respected as required by the constitution.

PROPOSITION FOR AN IMMIGRATION LAW

Contrary to the radical left media making people believe that Trump is anti-migrants-foreigners, it is archly false. As far as we are concerned, it is absurd to think that way given that Ivanka and Melania Trump are foreigners! Concerning illegal migrants, it is false again!

The fact is, if anyone wants to come to this country, there is a process of law to follow whether you decide to come either as a permanent alien, tourist, or political asylum. In all the countries in the world, even the poorest ones, have an immigration law.

It's not a secret. There is always an immigration law dealing with the status of people, namely if yes or not they are in conformity with the law. Why not also here in the United States? Also, do you agree with the way a whole avalanche of drug dealers, delinquents, children, and women abusers are entering our country? Is your memory failing you so badly, that you can't remember 9-11 where the worst terrorist attack occurred in the United States more precisely in the Capital of the world, New York City. Such a barbarous terrorist action has affected us both in materials and human lives. As a consequence, not only did it take us almost 15 years to rebuild it, but also a whopping amount of 10 billion dollars. So taking harsh measures that people are identified before being accepted into this country is racism and discrimination?

Nevertheless, it remains to know how Donald Trump would proceed to concretize a dream?

According to statistics collected from the period of 2017-2018, approximately 16 to 29 million people have illegally lived in the United States. Also, given this flurry of vested benefits from Biden's don't care policy during this recent past, we could estimate that number to be at least varied between 35 to 40 million illegal people in this country. Let's consider the highest number, given that many more should have entered without being caught and identified by the concerned service, which is HMS.

Wow! What such a defict balance for the United States! 49 million illegal people eat every day to the detriment of 180 million taxpayers of the country while working under the table and getting paid the same way. Therefore, it should be noted that at the same time people illegally entered this country, the Biden administration has set up a humanitarian immigration program in the following four countries: Venezuela, Cuba, Nicaragua, and Haiti.

Those four countries in question are entitled to 30,000 visas each month in the country. Since it began, about seven months ago it seems something is fishy because according to recent statistics, after 7 months, the number of people expected is quite far from being real. A total of 132,000 thousand have been accepted while the number is supposed to be 840,000 thousand. It should also be noted that 19 states, including Florida, are already camped crossfire against this program. So, trying not to include these 132,000 legally thousand entered, we only use 40 million people working without paying any tax!

Will the Social Security Institution be able to maintain this protocol until the end? Seeing this. Observing very closely the damage and interest that this could cause in the lives of our elderly in the near future, one wonders if it is not a question of a serious, conscious, and competent leader of the caliber of Donald J. Trump who takes charge of this, later will be sadder for the majority of our retired citizens, more especially our veterans who already, currently speaking, are living from hand to mouth.

Talking about an immigration reform for the USA is talking about a revolution in this area, to categorically fill the great void left by the Biden administration and replace it by a fair and adequate plan that responds well to the desires of this country.

First of all, to be eligible for a temporary green card, you must never commit any felony or more than three misdemeanors during all the period you have been illegally living in the country.

Secondly, having paid taxes and filing your tax return annually.

In case you never paid taxes, at the time where Donald Trump will sign the bill to become law, not only must you have a job, but also a 5% will be deducted every week on your paycheck while 10% on your return every year. You will have a period of 5 years to finish paying the penalty. Otherwise, until you have paid your debt, you will not be in possession of your green card.

Thirdly, for these young adults who want to go pursue their studies, given they are a temporary status to work, they still can go to school, but they will not be eligible for any loan or grant from the government until their penalty has been paid off.

Fourth, anyone, although reaching retiring age, will not be able to do so until the penalty is completely paid.

It should be important to notify that no matter what you religiously pay your fees, you must avoid committing any felony which will not only disqualify you, but also make you a real candidate for deportation after you are found guilty.

Fifth, for those belonging to DAKAR, given during all the period of incertitude, they used to work, go to school since they paid their bills in case there was one, they suppose benefit from legal status and American citizenship in case they wish to become Americans.

With such an adequate immigration reform, President Trump will be able to correct all past errors of the Biden administration to make America secure and great again. As far as the cost and economic return, it will be a great victory in this area for the country, especially since these profit figures will be able to speak for themselves. Let's try to mathematically analyze them globally to get an idea of his profitability in the state fund.

According to statistics mentioned above, about 40 million must pay their fair share for all the time living illegally without paying taxes. A 5% is perceived on the paycheck of everyone.

Let's take an income average of 400 dollars a week, at 5% which gives a total of 20 dollars per week. So, 40,000,000 x 20 = 800 million dollars per week or 41 billion six hundred million dollars (41,600,000,000) a year. What about the 10% on their return, the number is not quite easy to be accurate given that mathematics is an exact science. Anyway, to avoid empty space, we have judged it necessary to base ourselves on approximation, not on exactness. It is just to give us an idea of the return to the state coffers in this concern.

Most of these people are hardworking workers who most often earn minimum wages. Let's imagine they receive a return of 500 dollars from the IRS. From this return, they have to pay a 10% penalty of 50 dollars. So 40,000,000 × 50 = 2 billion dollars. So, choosing and opting for such immigration reform will endow the country not only with reliable and adequate economic relief, but also with correct security measures.

In this time, Americans' eyes will be wide open to recognize and make a great difference, seeing that Biden and his team were their biggest enemies when they housed illegal migrants of all types in luxurious hotels at an exorbitant cost, whether around more than 150 dollars the day of which nobody knows for how long these exorbitant contracts in question.

Meanwhile, the majority of our senior citizens live from

hand to mouth, not to say reduced to begging. Thus, towards such an economic revolution in this regard, Donald Trump will be able to make American people identify their true friends and enemies. He will also make them recognize the true face of the corrupt oligarchs whose main objective is to always prevent them from realizing their American dream by living a decent life with their family.

Finally, this great achievement with an approximation of an annual revenue of forty-three billion six hundred million (43,600,000,000) dollars will mean a magnificent victory of Americanism over globalism with Donald J. Trump, the main Architect-Builder-Director. Also, it should be noted that a temporary visa program will be set up each year on the agricultural level to meet the needs of our Farmers during the harvest period. You will come to work in the United States for a period of time starting from April to September, which is six months and is subject to being renewable each year. When the period of harvest is over, you must leave the United States to return to the fold unless your boss would like to use you for other services or other legal means entitling you to a green card. However, during your six months of temporary work, avoid committing any felonies because once occurred, you will not be able to set foot in the United States during the harvest.

DIFFERENCE IN LEADERSHIP AND GOVERNANCE BETWEEN DONALD TRUMP AND JOE BIDEN

Although knowing an ending spectacularly disastrous with a pandemic initiated by our number one counterfeiter, China, Trump's Presidency may always be remembered for so many great accomplishments during his four years in power. Despite also playing defense against several plots, nationals and internationals, including radical left media working for the oligarchs whose main objective is to collapse Americanism, it was for the first time that promises made, promises kept by a President in the United States.

According to researchers carried out, we are talking about thirty major projects concretized and executed by the Trump administration during his four hard years of mandate at the head of the country. So, you imagine a Donald Trump who did not face all these obstacles, starting with protests of defunding the police, passing by two false impeachments to end up with China's Covid-19 to name only those three, the United States would have dominated more the entire world. But unfortunately, it is sad that Trump has been trapped not only by many hypocrites of the country surrounding him, but also by the big tough enemies overseas.

The Trump administration has been notified by so many achievements that it is difficult to list them all in one book.

However, to have an idea, we are content to list a few. Unlike Obama who practiced a monovalent policy in which health insurance was his priority. It is true, this system during the recession had created almost two million jobs, but it also did a lot of harm to many working class where sanctions were multiplied against them, especially at the end of the year when it was a question of the IRS where your return was subject to heavy sanctions. Then imagine that it was a recession time where jobs were difficult to find any place.

So many people worked three months, six months expecting a return while being sanctioned for not having been enlisted in Obamacare. But as far as Donald Trump, knowing biblically speaking that man does not live by bread alone, once sworn in, he did start practicing what is called polyvalence, that is to say, approach all sectors of the country to create jobs. It paid off as the unemployment rate approximately varied between 3.4 and 3.7 percent.

As mentioned above, although a four-year long storm of rallies and on-air rants that ended in a mob riot, historic pandemic, and second impeachment, many Americans will always remember that there was more to the Trump presidency often unnoticed than attention hogging political drama and conflict. Thus, in the eyes of everyone, it is a fact that Trump and his administration actually did succeed in some ways changing the traditional system of Washington functioning under the leadership of the corrupt oligarchs and lobbyists. First of all, he did impose a ban on Chinese-made drones to rule back rules on sexual harassment. President Trump also changed some key areas of federal policy in ways that may have lasting impact well after he's gone.

Therefore, one of the principal strike forces of the Trump administration relied on its defense strategy to thwart notorious enemies. It is in this sense Trump refocused national security on great power competition. For Trump, our system of defense must be an exciting passage to camp quite solid to be capable of letting our adversaries know that we can not only defend ourselves but also our allies in case it should be necessary. Defense policy documents were so abundant that they could wallpaper Pentagon!

In this optic, Trump's national defense strategy and security stands out as the most important defense policy shifted of the last generation network correcting and reorienting the American military to confront rising and increasingly aggressive powers, Russia and China. What Biden supposed to follow to keep the United State of America Master and the Lord in this domain. Unfortunately, for some reason that we are about to understand, Joe Biden opted for bitter critics against Trump whom he said spread out the division all over the world instead of following the same path he took to make us stronger, he has judged opportune to do the opposite.

Therefore, as history is an eternal start over again, perhaps one day, he would face judgment of history for this wickedness committed and his lack of patriotism to the nation.

Regarding immigration, whether we like it or not, Trump has redeemed the country from notorious drug dealers and criminals of Salvador, Venezuela, Mexico, and special envoys of China. It is not without reason that Trump had broken the record in this area. Also, we believe by this new legislation of 2025, President Donald Trump will be able to easily solve this problem, which details were provided above. As for Biden, we stick a minus F on his back for his scam and immigration disorder created in the country during his leadership.

If well before, we were talking about 150 dollars daily per immigrant for a room at Ramada Hotel Up State New York, the cost is almost triple in Manhattan, whether about 1,750,000 dollars a day. They have such money, instead of issuing a check of 230 million for a period of six months, they made 250 million dollars. Why a bonus of 20 billion dollars to the hotel? Thus, the big question to ask is, does the hotel belong to the City? We highly doubt it. So it is not without reason that Biden administration leaves the field widely open to illegal immigrants, especially since we spend blindly without taking into account the accounting reports evaluating these frivolous expenses in question. That's one reason why they will never want Trump to be in control. Those oligarchs already know that he will never tolerate these kinds of shenanigans from them. Thus, for your memory and your archives, many responsible Americans were surprised, and at the same time angry to hear New York senator, Charles Schumer, answer a reporter's question about the hundreds of thousands of illegal migrants invading the country through Biden policy, "it's nothing, it doesn't matter."

The senator in function answered as follows: "Well, listen to this, it has been a long time since we continued to show a deficit of fertility in this country. Thus, if it keeps going on this same path, it will be quite crucial and consequential for the United States. Therefore, we need migrants at all costs and in any case to fill the void. Wow, America!" Such was the answer of a senator representing a state considered the most flourishing and opulent in the world, whose role is to make the laws.

It's not without reason that true love doesn't exist anymore throughout the world, especially in the United States of America. Many men and women practice what is called: "We love each other, we have a good time, then we don't remember anything until we are thirsty for each other again!" But where the bottom hurts, it's the same senators of the caliber of Schumer's who favor abortion anytime and anyhow! Several Christian parents found it very bizarre, nasty, and quite abominable such an inappropriate statement of the radical left whose only objective is to turn the whole world upside down, more especially their own.

Therefore, still on this topic of migration, it should be noted for your memory that Bill Clinton, almost at last in his first term, was to in a statement before the Congress assume the right as president of the United States to explain the gravity of the situation in the country with the repeated avalanche of illegal migrants entering the country.

He was quoted: "To all Americans, to all of those in States more and less affected by the flood of illegal aliens storming your State, we are asking Congress, Democrats and

Republicans, to recognize and admit that drastic measures be taken to curb this caravan because it affects us in every way. I also recommend that efforts be doubled and reinforced in order to properly secure our borders to avoid the worst. Furthermore, I ask about illegal people to no longer have access to welfare assistants, and in the event of crimes, that they be deported as quickly as possible." In the follow he added: "Certainly, we are a country of migrants, but also, we must recognize and admit for true that we are a country governed by laws under the banner of which, we must base to make sure they are well applied and respected."

As a result, because of such a good action accomplished by President Clinton, the last was quite gifted by American people allowing him to greatly beat Bob Dole by more than 8 million votes and more than 379 electorates.

It is from this moment, we must recognize a serious and honest man of integrity in Donald Trump.

Bill Clinton is a Democrat while Donald Trump is a Republican. What could we have noticed almost 20 years ago, 1996 and 2017??

Donald, as an evolutionary, seeing that Clinton had realized an excellent job in this area, had judged opportune to follow the same path to make it more efficient and secure for this country where the number of hundreds of thousands who used to enter this country illegally was considerably reduced. Compared to what we are currently living in this regard, this is day and night. It's not a surprise, the same traditional left radical media and oligarchs who congratulated Bill Clinton, this is the same people who nicknamed Trump racist and divisionary when in their eyes Trump rendered the access of entering illegally in this country more difficult for people willing to violate the law. So, the problem is personal with Donald Trump. That's why the guy upstairs will always protect him for being a man of conviction, a leader who makes his promises to the American people while keeping them all!. No matter the party to which you belong to, this is the United States of America, you concretize something good for the country, Trump backs it up!

It is in this sense that he had taken into consideration the statement made before the Congress in 1996 to render it more disciplined, efficient and applicable in the eyes of everyone. But, despite it being often said that dirty linens are washed as a family, we can also understand that with time, everything could have changed. Can Bill Clinton agree with Biden's behavior in that regard?

However, don't be surprised that Bill Clinton is playing oblivion, forgetting his famous declaration before the Congress in 1996 to agree with Biden, especially if, like the latter, Bill Clinton's age brings unreason instead of reason.

Trump's success continued to do its merry way in the matter of tax cuts. Having said he's the representative of the voice of the voiceless, once sworn in, President Trump, had raised the standard deduction to a high level to allow the middle and hardworking class to be greatly relieved. Under the Obama administration, the standard deduction was 6,500 dollars, in his first term, it was already passed at 12,000 dollars. As a result, for the first time in the history of the United States, year 1998, 111 million Americans received from IRS each, a total of 2,869 dollars. Unfortunately, so many of those taxpayers, having been penalized because they did not enlist in the ObamaCare, had not received their check. In this context, who cares more about the poor in America?

Here we're about to approach the year of 2024. We do accuse a terrible inflation where the price of everything has quadrupled actually, but this standard deduction doesn't still move one inch! It remains the same as Trump rose it in 2018. So one must ask, who else is better than Donald Trump? Our youth is supposed to think with their brain, but not with their head. With the technology, you can see for yourself without leaving any corrupt media to induce you in error. We must not parody them if we want to move forward.

For them, gratefulness is cowardly, but for us, it must mean: knowing how to appreciate someone's good deeds and Donald Trump was and will be the one deserving this appreciation.

As far as education, Trump was one of the champions in this domain where a lot of reforms had taken place to make it adequate for the generation of the new millennium to benefit from it in order to be able to take over.

Trump boosted religious organizations in education. Although a little failure to enact any sweeping school choice policy that sends money to parents to help them pay for private and religious schools. But as someone who always opts for an adequate and successful pedagogical system in this field. It is in this sense that we found in the Trump administration an educational system led by the Education Secretary Betsy DeVos, a devout Christian who found a way to expand federal support for religious schools and organizations at the Education Department.

As a result, Secretary DeVos tweaked a wide range of education policies, large and small to boost faith-based organizations. She completely changed regulations, for example, to make it easier for members of religious orders to access federal financial aid and expand Federal Public Service Loan Forgiveness to cover clergy members.

She also created new protections for faith-based campus organizations at public universities. In regard to the K-12 education level, DeVos stopped enforcing a policy that had prohibited religious organizations from providing publicly funded services, such as tutoring, technology, and counseling in private schools. And one of the most important achievements in the domain of education was when she opened up federal grants for Charter Schools reserving a place for students with good behaviors and the desire to improve by getting good grades, it should be noted that those Charter Schools in play are often affiliated with religious organizations.

The fruit of her labor was so appreciated and rewarding that many religious education groups praised DeVos's changes as meritorious relief for an excellent education system in this country, which she personally often described as an expanded religious liberty. In this concern, she revealed that too many misinterpret the separation of church and state as an invitation for the government to separate people from their faith.

Therefore, a correct and successful system of this kind should serve as a model for the Biden Administration to continue on the same path for more success, unfortunately, all the good things accomplished by President Donald Trump have always bitter tastes for Biden whose hatred against that one remains as a towel that burns forever because he's a true enemy of the truth. Being a daredevil of first class full of tricks making promises he never can and always keep. Thus, renouncing his poor performance, shenanigans, and achievement during almost 40 years in the senate, to him, Trump is the principal black beast who deserves an infernal punishment.

But still, in 2025, after taking the oath, Trump would be able to call on this pedagogue with a very full and made head that of Mrs. Betsy to continue to restore the reputation of our education system for the greater good of the new generation calling for succession. We must give Caesar what belongs to him. President Trump, a fervent supporter of changing to evaluate, had placed all his trust in Secretary Betsy as very dynamic, competent, and serious to put in the trap of wasting state funds by approving loans anyhow to students even when not eligible.

It was a total waste of the state coffers from which the private technical institution for the most part was still the main beneficiary. We take as an example a particular case of a young woman who as a novice in this regard, has been forced to grant a loan of 30,000 dollars to become a medical assistant.

This young adult in question didn't even speak English! Who cares!? She also didn't know how to fill out a simple job application, because not wanting to continue with her medical assistant's class, she was looking for a factory job.

After only two weeks in class, she desperately wanted to quit! But she was told that she already registered and had signed up for this class. We couldn't change anything actually for being too late. The problem that arose was that she couldn't understand anything in the subjects she was being taught.

These kinds of situations repeated themselves throughout the period of the Obama-Biden Administration and that it was important and necessary for President Trump that Secretary Betsy was in charge of saving and redeeming them from the lawless liberals. In concert with the interior ministry, President Trump ordered Secretary Betsy DeVos to prevent loans from being granted to unqualified people. And it was well done.

If sometime there are discussions to know in which or what department the Trump administration had done better as long as successes were enormous. For many, agriculture would be the area where Trump excelled the most. But it depends on where you are located. For example, if you are drawn from the peasantry, you will see that agriculture with Donald Trump was a resounding success to be no longer comparable. However, in the area of defense, energy, education to only name a few.

As mentioned above it depends on the sector to which you belong. If they question truck or taxi drivers, they will tell you a thousand times that fuel energy is their priority regarding Trump's accomplishments because from 1.87 $ the gallon to 4.89 and 3.69 actually, that was a big relief, they advanced as proof. Unfortunately, time does not allow us to trace all the 30 projects carried out by Trump. But in the field of education, defense, agriculture, energy, economy and more especially, migration, compared to Biden, it is the day vs the night.

Until now, migrants continue to enter illegally. They have just reported that several tents are laying down in the city before a hotel which is already full of more than 3,000. Being packed and overcrowded, the hotel cannot accept any more illegal migrants. As a consequence, most of them said they had remained without food and without showers for 4 days. That's what President Biden gives to the American people as a gift.

AMERICANISM VS GLOBALISM

This is a thorny problem that Trump has always faced, that of combatting, which has a clearly globalist tendency. These people are camped crosswise in front of Donald Trump not only to defend their political agenda but also to impose their own law. Therefore, one might ask, how can a small group of oligarchies thwart Trump's programs for this country when one knows the latter is very popular, dragging behind him more than 75 million American voters?

The reason of the strongest is always the best. In this sense, to make an allusion to a biblical passage in this regard, formulating that man proposes while God disposes. We also deduce from it that 75 million Americans voted Trump while this skinny of the oligarchy hierarchy decided. Therefore, hoping that the concerned party won't play the same blind in 2024 so that every vote counts and that we never return to a situation similar to that of January 6, 2021.

The Americanism promoted by Trump is simple like good morning to understand. This is a question to make America great again. But to do so, drastic measures are necessary to thwart the one already existing, to combat by all means internal and external corruptions, the interference of the United States in nonsense conflicts of other countries.

Trump has quickly understood that it is the greatest avant-garde factor needed to do whatever you want to accomplish in the world.

However, when for some reason we trample into upside-down activities which cost our country in money and human lives, especially Americans, we will never be considered as a country that moves forward. So many examples are crystal clear before us to testify to it. An invasion in Iraq, Libya, Afghanistan will never be part of Trump's agenda.

Even when he started involving at an advanced age, that did not prevent him from observing so many collapses of the superpower countries to steep themselves up in a useless war, as a result, they have become in deficit in everything.

We can take as an example the Soviet Union in Afghanistan where after fierce fighting, considerable losses were recorded on both sides. As a result, the biggest beneficiary was the United States with a Ronald Reagan all fire, all flames who profited from the joke of Gorbachev, namely: he himself knocked down the wall. Despite everything, that did not prevent George W. Bush from failing to commit the same error to notice his influence of global globalization which unfortunately had so soaked the country because Wall Street was for the first time registered such a low record.

Even today, although not physically immersed in this war in Ukraine, we can see that it has just already caused this last inflation that the United State knows currently because billions of dollars of our taxpayers including heavy weapons and equipment are already released and dispersed to help Ukraine deal with the war.

What President Donald Trump does not without doubt digest quite well to make him say: that it is always better to prevent than to cure. This is still the great difference between him and the others. How to waste billions of dollars of our people while these same people live from hand to mouth, not to say in filth.

Trump is not the only one thinking that way. Anyone with a good common sense and vision for this country must meditate large and profoundly to say that it cannot continue that way. The country is about to lose its value.

On this particular segment, whether you are a Democrat or Republican, if you really love the United States, don't ask this country what it can keep doing for you, of preference, ask yourself how to contribute to allow this country that you so cherish to be what it was before.

If you are truly an Americanophile, you must have the courage to recognize and admit for true that something is currently freaky and fishy. A crucial situation which is not supposed to be only a Democrat concern or preoccupation. It should be the concern of all conscious and consistently proud of the beauty and grandeur of their country. Therefore, the Democrat leader R.F. Kennedy Jr. probably does not share the same ideology and political vision as Donald Trump, but as far as mad war, inflation, environment, and many others, they share almost the same opinion for an adequate solution to end the crisis.

He continued to say that he cares less about only 15% supporting his vision for this country. However, he believes, as relative to Kennedy's family whose father Robert Kennedy, studying profoundly political concept, he's sure and certain it was a true vision identifying the Democratic Party. It's the true best for America contrary to what we are experiencing actually.

This guy, although having been victimized by a stroke in 1996, 27 years later, that does not prevent him from retaining an elephant memory to remember everything. What Trump considers as someone with good lucidity to see that Democrats are destabilizing and destroying this country. With proofs in hand, he also declares that there is no way to play blindfolded and turn a deaf ear when statistics have revealed, in black and white, that the United States has been borrowing respectively 1 billion dollars each day from China and Japan. Do they let the American people know that the war in Iraq cost us 8 trillion dollars? Did our fellow Americans know that the China-Covid19 cost us 16 trillion dollars? What about the current war in Ukraine? When will it end? We do not have a magic wand to make such a prediction. However, it has already cost us 113 billion so far. While 25% of American people are not even living from hand to mouth but in extreme poverty, not to say filth.

In this context, an alarm bell is proving extremely necessary for a smart-led awakening to tell the Biden Administration: DON'T YOU DARE! THE UNITED STATES OF AMERICA IS NOT FOR SALE TO CHINA.

UNITED STATES OF AMERICA BELONGS TO THE AMERICAN PEOPLE

It is good news for this country to see both Democrats and Republicans admit that the country has taken a very bad direction with Joe Biden. It's not without reason that the President's acolytes try to hide him under the basement, avoiding debates to shed light and allowing American people to know what's really going on. Being always great enemies of lies, Schumer, Pelosi, and so many potential Democrats are camping in crossfire to prevent these debates from taking place.

Can they always be successful? We don't think so. This time, for people to understand that they made a bad choice, it's against them who pay the consequence in return. Actually, the cat is out of the bag. There is no way for the Democrats to put the blame on Trump, whom they say hates foreigners to be in the United States because their brother put it crystal clear for them that no any other countries in the world will accept more than 7 million migrants of all kinds enter their country without a legal process determining the legitimacy of those people in question because such an hustle and bustle entry and penetration of most those criminals further aggravates this thorny crisis that the United States is facing today.

Whether the way R.F. Kennedy Junior would like to express, it's as if the country is already mortgaged.

Now, whether we like it or not, the cat is already out of the bag. There's no more hidden game. For this reason, one compares Biden to a car on a muddy hill where there are cliffs to the right and to the left. All this is to say, agreeing to debate R.F. Kennedy Jr. is already a severe crick in legs for Biden, while not accepting to debate means every monkey business told about him is more than true. Thus, on both sides, the harm is infinite.

AMERICA FIRST!

For this new generation of students, more especially, hardworking youth Americans, your Donald Trump is a real fighter who always wants to work hard without getting weary and tired to allow the country to take flight like an eagle towards the destiny of the climax. Also, a true patriot who, since his youth until the present moment, has always been in favor of the full interest of the American people and swears to always defend it, these interests tooth and nail for the full return of the country he loves and cherishes so much. It is in this sense, we often hear him said to the youth of this country that the fight does not start yesterday and today. It's a long fight for which, I, DONALD TRUMP, have always been an avant-garde to denounce all uses of most of our allies in concert with traditional territorial politicians that have made our hardworking taxpayers suffer.

Currently, it is not without reason that Donald Trump represents and considers being the main enemy who prefers to destroy him instead of trying to help him to defend tooth and nail the interest of the nation. Unfortunately, this is quite badly calculated by his opponents because if defending the interest of the United States of America is a crime, instead of condemning him for classified and declassified documents, indict him for being too careful and too patriotic! Don't be afraid, the Architect says! We, Americans, do not learn how to fight, we are born fighters. These are words, not only does he mean it but also signs it up, too, in capital letters.

As pointed out way back above, Trump has always been treated as a divisor and racist by the left because he always stands up to take in open hands the defense of American taxpayers and the hardworking middle class. Therefore, what his eternal political opponents need to know is that Trump is far from all of these bitter critics. Then, the day when American people really understand what good leadership means, they will surely not agree to apply and put into consideration the left, the anarchic, and the liberal policy of the Democrats who are often doomed to failure, alluding to Jimmy Carter and currently Joe Biden.

In 2019, they made Dr. Trump responsible for all the problems facing the country without having the good memory to remember that they were the ones being at first for all these problems because from the day Donald Trump swore in until December 19, 2019, when China felt the dizzying rise of the spectacular growth of our economy, sees fit to threaten us with this China's Covid-19, including defund the police, two impeachments of the left to prevent Trump from keeping his promises to the American people and achieve his goal for this country. But despite everything, his administration had set several records in terms of good governance. Because of all these good things, there are several tens of thousands of Americans who have not hidden their satisfaction to establish the great difference between the administration of Donald Trump and the one in which we are currently floundering, trampling, and plowing. Their good sense of reason has allowed them to distinguish between fine words and actions where they are facing the reality of the facts.

As far as beautiful words and promises, Trump said we have listened to them for over forty years until the state of August 22, 2020, when they uttered the shocking nonsense negative words in the ears of the American people. Trump did not hesitate even a fraction of a second to say, "My dear fellow Americans, wake up! We don't want to go back to the failed policy of Obama Care which has caused a lot of headaches and stresses to American people, especially the minority where until 2019, according to two left media whose names I'm careful not to mention, penalties were applied to them for not having enrolled.

As a consequence, many taxpayers didn't still receive their returns from the IRS including their Stimulus check on time because they have been penalized for not having ridden with Obama in his health care socialist policy.

At almost three or four crossroads, there is a school in the United States! How did the Democrats think people are stupid and mindless not to understand their tricky games often at play?

For this particular topic, a retrospective return is necessary.

When all the same leaders such as Pelosi, Schumer, President Obama, Biden see themselves as champions and staunch defenders of the working class, these are only words that wind blows away and blow outside the doorstep of those poor people they claim to be the personal savior of.

They knew that the sky was not blue at all, but they made you believe it was. This is what is called caressing hypocrites with deceitful faces. We would say this is what they do to make a living: that of telling people they do care about them, they are always by their side for a better living condition. It was not without reason that Trump had gone to the battlements to enlighten these innocent people with this famous phrase: "Ladies and gentlemen, always and everlasting the same nonsense talks and false promises for over forty years to wash people's brains and make them accept chicken poops for eggs."

It is suchly evident, let's try to go back to 2019. So, a pandemic had already begun to rage. The Republicans were already opting for a bill of twelve hundred dollars US of relief for people in need, more importantly, those the most vulnerable whose savings accused negative balances. But what happened? Asked Trump.

Two or three months later, the Democrats were still slow to address the issue of people starving to death and did not move an inch, while these same people, whom they claimed to defend, suffered bitterly. Despite the great determination of the Republican Senate to quickly move forward, we could easily observe the Democrats on the other side playing the politics of marronage, not only to kill time but also to tarnish, as we said before, the image of Donald Trump as a bad leader and to raise the people against him during a terrible and crucial time for the country.

To make people judge for themselves, President Trump had to be accompanied all the time by a pen, in full conference, to tell Americans: "I'm ready, right now! Bring me the bill also signed by Democrats! I'll stop the meeting to sign it!" Trump went further to say, "Anytime, everywhere, even when being in bed, bring me the bill, I shall sign it!"

As I noticed, it was since May the bill was on the table; we're actually in September! I want you to understand that I have done everything within my reach to pass four bills allowing you to face your financial challenge in a moment quite crucial for you and your family. Actually, it's up to Democrats to play their part. They must stop playing dirty games to unblock your financial situations. They are in the majority. It's time for them to move from promise to action.

In any case, as a President who is always concerned with your problems, I reiterated that I will always be ready to sign the bill. My Republican supporters in the Senate and Congress are only waiting for the signal from the opposite side to do the same. It is not without reason that it is no secret that Trump's popularity has risen and grown to mind-boggling numbers because the cat is out of the bag actually. These leftists have been caught hand in the bag by most of their partisans during bad feeding businesses. The evidence is too clear and tangible. That's why the American people are saying currently they are fed up with these cow s*it leaders who pamper them in appearance and in flattering words while deep down dragging them into misery so as not to even think about realizing the American dream.

In this context, a lot of arguments and discussions are currently taking place among them, especially passionate Democrats and independents, too!

It is not a surprise to see people are really concerned about Biden's politics. What's even worse and puts the oil into the fire is the opinion of the Republican candidate, Nikki R. When she said that Biden knows full well he's a one-term candidate, but he tries to play who loses wins. He has nothing. He will be eighty years old in 2024. Thus, despite his managerial weakness and his unpopularity across all the fifty states of the United States, he no longer takes into account! He has become a true daring leader, as he has always been, full of cunning to throw himself mercilessly, 2023-2024 into the event that same electoral shenanigans occur and Biden is elected President of the United States, shortly after his inauguration, he will declare he will step out and entrust power to his vice-president who has always been loyal to him.

Therefore, for all these reasons enumerated well before, it should be taken into account but badly calculated because people don't like Kamala. In other words, she's not competent at all! The only way they would accept her to lead the party, it's if the White House was a comedy theater where people laugh time after time. Then as far as that, she would have been the champion.

For among people, accepting Kamala for being the next president of this country, it is coming out of a one-eyed man to join a blind woman. As far as Democratic voters, who are mostly middle class, there is total panic and dissatisfaction. They claim to be ready to reverse the situation in 2023 even when they would be able to choose a serious and competent Democratic candidate to discourage Biden by forcing him to pack up before the end of his term.

Also, even though many TRUMPETS have said that NIKKI HALEY has greatly misled them, choosing to face TRUMP in 2024, instead of waiting for 2028 to have the latter's full support. However, it must be recognized that the statement expressed by her in this regard makes a lot of sense. But Trumpist voters in concert with independents and some moderates have already decided Biden's fate. Whether they like it or not, his election funeral will be held on November 5, 2024. But in all of this, according to polls, Dr. Donald Trump is on the right slope because comparing his spectacular rise to power crowned with laurels by good governance, people say what good has Biden done for us?

A vertiginous inflation! A sorceress economy! An insecure border giving free access to millions of notorious criminals, children, and drug traffickers to enter our soil with no hesitation and fear! A remarkable weakness in our military capacity exciting and encouraging China to provoke us and behave like Master and Lord! An unequaled and incomparable avalanche of corruption in collusion with overseas enemies, of which the hierarchical head of the bridge is a party and has placed himself at the top of the list!

For all these reasons, the American people have deemed it urgent to take a final resolution to no longer want to go where Biden would like to continue to lead the country, 2024-2028. The latter go on to say that if the will of the people is the one that decides and prevails, to avoid making the same mistake of the past, we all, Republicans, Independents, and Moderate Democrats will board the 2024 flight of MAGA to MASSIVELY VOTE DONALD TRUMP.

TOO ALL AMERICANS ELIGIBLE TO VOTE

By Mr 1WONDERFUL1

Voters, when your balance sheet during your time in New Jersey was super and ultra-negative! That was in 2015. What about now? It's from bad to worse because after an 8-year lay-off, Crist was still inactive in this field, except for his coming and going to CNN, NBC to brutally tackle Donald Trump; there is nothing more! Accordingly, it is time for C.C. to go to learn how to fish or golf because a good recipe in 2023-2024 remains a very long shot, not to say an impossible mission for MISTER CRIST ON EARTH.

The latter must know, once for all, if he can't click, he's not fit. If he's not fit, he must quit for DONALD TRUMP, the best BAND LEADER of the field to make MAGA. CRIST must also remember, just as genius is often said to be a miracle only a century. So, after Barack Obama, we must be patient to wait for another 94 years, whether in 2194 MUSTER!

As a result, we urge all Americans to always have good memories so as not to forget like Chris, the good deeds of Donald Trump, who despite all the suffering endured, wanted to do everything in his capacity to respect all the promises he made to you in 2016. You all are ocular witnesses, the strength, the will, the knowledge, all were there for a job to be well done. Unfortunately, even his own partisans had contributed to try to sink his ship of changes. Let's not forget on CNN specifically, his number one enemy media, he said: as always, when I'm elected President, I shall be the President of all Americans, especially the often forgotten men and women. I also promise to be the main representative of the voice of the voiceless in the United States of America. To do so, my credo is Americanism in its entirety, and not globalism. The words go away, but the writing always remains indelible forever.

These were the promises to the American people without distinction. Perhaps, it is undoubtedly what made these traditional leaders panic to prevent the Trumpest revolution from being a total success either for the voiceless people or the country. It is in this sense, one might say they used all the clever stratagem to seal it off in Pennsylvania and Georgia. However, since the roots of MAGA are deep and numerous, they will grow back in greater numbers on November 5, 2024.

As an evolving people, of bravery and magnanimity, we must never forget that a people without historical memory is a people without a future. Don't just tell us what you're going to do to alleviate our misery. Please tell us what you have already accomplished for the American people. In response to such a question, among all of them, Donald Trump is the only one who can claim the right to say: I HAVE ALREADY ACCOMPLISHED A LOT AND PROMISED TO DO MUCH BETTER IN THE DAYS TO COME.

AFTERWORD

It's not a secret to anyone that our country has always been, and still is, currently in peril. Given this bad state into which this country has plunged, it is imperative that things must inevitably change for the United States to regain its right as the greatest, number one nation, accepted and undisputed.

The first nation in the world to serve as a compass and a key example to allow democracy and peace to bud and grow all over the planet on earth. Thus, all this objective is only Donald Trump's wish for our country to be able to set up this good example.

Donald Trump, the speaker for the voice of the voiceless, conceives of a country that claims to be number one, must be number one in the true sense of the word. For the latter, we can count several hundred millionaires and tens of billionaires among us.

But what about the voice of the voiceless who daily live from hand to mouth? To be a real number one in all its entirety, without being socialist, we must allow all Americans to be able to lead a decent life. Otherwise, our educational system will experience catastrophic fallout and generate heinous crimes that will be difficult to stop.

It was not without reason, as mentioned above, given how hard class people were victimized by Obamacare insurance, punishing them for over three years when it was questioned about their return income from the IRS. Thus, Donald Trump, once sworn in in 2017, not only cut taxes as promised but also increased the standard deduction to allow those belonging to the low class to pay their debts regarding penalties imposed by the Obama administration. That way, the Standard Deduction was passed from $6,500 to $12,500, such has been a big increase by Donald Trump. As a result, 111 million taxpayers, for the most, received a return of $2,869.

It's not without reason that Trump always says, because I choose to be your representative, they prosecute me by trying all the ways to silence me and prevent Americanism from prevailing over globalism. It's very unfortunate that people, not knowing more than the tip of their nose, think that they can counter what decides beyond.

All these indictments, which are about to happen, had to happen. It is from November 5, 2024, that people will stop behaving to only believe when they see. Besides, it's started already, that is to say, someone being accused of all kinds of bad behaviors, while this someone in question, on this election board, jumps higher than all his opponents in the number of thirteen of them to be the avant-garde candidate, passing and trailing behind him all others at an imaginable and incredible distance, including Joe Biden or any other Democratic candidate they would tend to take over in case where President Joe Biden would be putting in a state of weakness to press his luck for another four years of turmoil and disaster.

In this optic of ideas, we would deduce that God created human beings different from each other. Donald Trump, without doubt, would also be this preferential creation from the Lord's mind, incarcerating within him such an ability to fight and overcome obstacles he has been and is always faced these days.

Once again, don't we see the difference regarding his strength to remain firm and solid although tide and storms threaten him? Can't we see that he's never being afraid because, as the pre-classic French writer, Francois De Villon, he would not mind to say: I'm Donald J. Trump, all the pleasure is mine to let you know to whom willing to hear it: Do as you wish if you still decide to win without peril and triumph with no glory.

However, I want to point it out to you. On behalf of the voice of the voiceless of which I'm the main defender and also for whom I decide to fight until the end, the Master who has always taken care of my youth did not never teach me how to kneel down to ask forgiveness from those who are already guilty for themselves.

Still, wisdom demands that we appeal to the faculty of patience and belief to obtain the key to the treasure. Trump's philosophy has always taught him that a true leader and Americanophile is considered as such, when he or she must have patience to work hard in order to be successful. Otherwise, this so-called is like a lamp without the oil. But it's unfortunate this is what we are currently experiencing in Washington where the corrupt oligarchs ignore all the sacrifices of our martyr heroes to endow us with a great and free country. Thus, either out of political and economical ambition or above all, have agreed to take it to the enemy at a low price. These, to repeat after the author in question, are real lamps without the actual oil. Fortunately, any prayer has always an AMEN!

Today, in sporting reference where the Lakers, warriors were shipwrecked against the Denvers. Also today like women's soccer, FIFA World Cup 2023, in which the big tenors like Germany, Italy, Brazil were respectively eliminated by small ones like Jamaica, Morocco, and South Korea, it will be the same politically speaking on November 5, 2024, where the voices of the voiceless go to the polls in droves to vote and elect Donald J. Trump President of the United States of America. And this, not only for their relief in all kinds, but also for the greatest goods of the country that come out under the tutelage of the corrupt national and international oligarchs.

In this context, it should be noted that politics is like a

species of cocaine addiction by Hunter. This substance killer is so strong that it can cause the latter or anyone else consuming it to act on instinct without considering the harmful consequences that come in return. It is not without reason that shenanigans businesses with China, Ukraine, Romania, and so many others have been honored to the detriment of the American people without the perpetrators of these notorious crimes also thinking that one day they should be on the bench of the defendants to testify.

That's why, being traumatized with such an addiction makes them completely ignore that Donald Trump is someone who is called and entrusted by this invisible force to accomplish this mission. Thus, whoever wants to hinder him and throw him in prison will pay the consequence of non-respect towards the one who entrusted him with this mission.

So, do we need to experience more vision to see a bit of similarity between the Master and his special envoy who is Donald Trump? Thus, if after all these miracles were performed, the Jews had not still recognized that Jesus was not an ordinary person, it would be the same for these oligarchs to not also take into account the drove popularity of Donald Trump to not condemn him for history being an eternal beginning. However, what is painful in this phase of history, it will be the whole country which will be paying for this fiasco in case Donald Trump should not be elected President of the United States on November 5, 2024. But this doubt has not its place since it is already written black on white that Trump is guided by Beyond. It is also revealed that there is a big connection between Donald Trump and the one we try to forget about.

According to the same revelation, Christians and the voice of the voiceless will be unified to become a mighty force not to be reckoned with. For this particular reason, Trump's sacrificers will only have one option: that of packing up and conceding defeat by consciously admitting for sure that the will of the people is the will of God. And no matter the tides or storms, it is unavoidable. In this context, when this happens, light will be seen to pour all over the nation, not leaving even a sliver of space for the darkness to settle.

At this time, we will see that his master will help him make the wise choice of serious and competent people, unlike in 2017 when his own collaborators plotted against him to prevent him from accomplishing, in the true sense of the term, what was entrusted to him for the Americans, more specifically the voice of the voiceless that he represents and for whom also, he dedicates himself until the end. On this point of view, we had learned before that being a frank patriot and loyal was a sign of treason against a country which provides all the necessary tools to become congressmen, Senators, President, and even women soccer's players the best paid of the world. There's a book called: CIVIC INSTRUCTION.

This was a little book from which students in third grade have learned how to serve and respect their country. Given how most Americans' bad behaviors in this regard actually, if this is no longer served, it should be an obligated passage to allow it to resurface for the generation of the new millennium because we have seen it disappear, such a pride especially when it is a matter to salute and pay respect to our flag, which is the emblem of our nation. That's the main reason so many of those calibers are anti-Trumpets because it's an aberration quite disgusting to see the majority of the American women Soccer players refuse to salute and sing the American ANTHEM! They called Trump Diversionary!

How to ask Donald to turn a deaf ear and play blindfold towards such an anti-patriotic gesture while the whole world is watching?

On this, it should be noted that a goalkeeper from a Banana Republic, whom we remain anonymous, thus, despite being a very good goalkeeper, had to spend more than three months begging for a visa to enter Australia to participate and represent her country. Finally, three days before the starting of this competition, she had collected that visa in question. But despite everything, she was the first player to stand up to salute the flag of her country and sing the national anthem with joy and pride. It's very shameful to observe such dirty behavior. What message does that spread through the world? The USA is the main pet peeve, betrayed by its own players. And as President, if it's that way, they will never be welcome to the White House.

Therefore, for your comprehension and archives, the United States National women's soccer team is the most successful women's team in the history of the women's world cup. Having won four titles of nine, they have always been considered as such. A difficult opponent to beat. They also earned second place once and three third places. Unfortunately, everything was overwhelming in Australia as our team struggled to reach the second round to be eliminated by Sweden. It is for the first time not only Sweden beat the USA in a FIFA World Cup, but also eliminated them for the rest of the competition, preventing them from reaching the third round.

According to sources that we can trust, this team didn't receive the full support of the fans after several criticisms were multiplied against the majority of the players having been mean to the flag.

On this particular issue, we seize the opportunity to bitterly criticize the writer Linehan, special envoy in the circumstance. What people must know is that there is a big difference between a reporter and a historian. The reporter is often partial.

What we must understand is that Linehan is not a historian to report the fact as it is. She, too, is part of the team for which she was the speaker. By saying that, fans don't have a problem with singing the anthem or flag matters. The problem has to be seen with gender, pedophilia, to name a few. Is it false when we know that any time the team enters the field the crowd never has ever traded their applause for the players. The question of preference or sectarian affiliation of the players under the color of the pen of Linehan has no place in this situation. Thus, the words go away but the writing and images remain. According to images, it is unique and simple, just like several baseball and basketball players, some of Megan Rapinoe's followers had deemed necessary to abstain during the salute of the flag. But in this situation, Congress has to act quickly to formulate a law that stipulates: any American athlete who decides not to salute the flag of this country cannot represent the UNITED STATES.

As far as Donald Trump, who loves the game and also used to play it too, his patriotic sentiment didn't allow him to watch the team. According to the same source, he would have advanced as arguments. If the own band leader of this country is careless about its sovereignty, how do you ask soccer players to even care when first-class oligarchs want by all means to liquidate it to enemies? What about Megyn Kelly, a journalist patriot, she goes far to turn her TV off not to watch the game because I don't support hate and anti-Americanism.

"I hope they will lose," she added, to show her anger and at the same time make her spirit of patriotism and love for the country felt. However, a challenge is launched. All those who want to sully the image of the country, whether in the sporting, social, or political field, will have a price to pay. Recently, it has just happened from a sporting viewpoint. Thus, from a political one, on November 5, 2024, it will be more consequential when these troublemakers and hierarchical oligarchs of all kinds are already planning to sow terror in the circumstance. This time, it will not be soccer fans to whom they will face, but this invisible force, ALPHA and OMEGA. The one who already decides that the light be shed on November 5, 2024. The one who has the power to move mountains with the wave of a gentle hand and cross seas with a gentle whisper.

All is good enough to convince that in the face of danger, Donald J. Trump will have no fear. According to the one formulating once again seven times: that the light shines in the United States of America. Thus, it is an acquired fact. The key to the White House is already handed over to President Donald Trump to bring the country back to safety and make it great again.

Therefore, as a country like no other, it is in our interest to do everything in our power to prevent our Hero, George Washington, from shaking with anger and dying again in the grave because he bravely fought to leave us a country full of honor and glory. A country with a vocation for leadership in the world. Not a country to be under the yoke of the tutelage of other countries, such as China and Russia, to only name these two. Anyone having a good sense of reason must know that the United States has been experiencing a shameful and turmoil situation, acute since Biden came to power. It is no longer a secret that the country is in peril, which inexplicably demands a solution by a leader who is competent and honest but also one who has the sense of patriotism welling up in his veins at the caliber of Donald Trump, who already has his plan well traced to a resurrection in the manner of Jesus, that of snatching out wonderful USA from the clutch of national and international oligarchs on January 20, 2025.

This is a mistake to be avoided. As explained above, there is a bit of similarity between Trump's policy and the little Jacobin Noir of the 17th century, Napoleon Bonaparte, who did not understand the importance of this charismatic leader for the interest of France, had to deport him, humiliate him and imprison him, then came his death, quite asphyxiated. However, when the latter felt completely beaten, he finished recognizing and admitting for true that the biggest mistake he had ever made during his leadership was the sentence inflicted on Toussaint Louverture (little Jacobin Noir).

For this particular reason, American people must know that history is an eternal restart. But also, a people without historical memory is a people without a good future. So as not to be like Great Napoleon, if we knew that Donald Trump was the most suitable leader for a great America again, we would have voted for him. But time lost never made up.

Refresh your memory to see that Donald Trump was good for the country, more especially for the middle class and the voice of the voiceless. Do we need to be a number cruncher to know about that? When going to the supermarket, filling up for a tank of fuel, also taking a look at our savings account, to name a few. Don't we see that we are completely in deficit and that four more years of President Biden in the White House will completely plunge us into the hole not to resurface to realize our American Dream?

Avoid the repetition of such a mistake by choosing Donald Trump to correct all these blunders created by the Biden Administration to replace them with a system suitable for the American people where Americanism will have the honor while triumphing magnificently, leaving aside the globalism orchestrated by corrupt oligarchs, which instead of helping the people of this country, preferably stick together with the international enemies to plunge them into darkness.

Nevertheless, even when the fate of the country already rests in the hands of the supreme being, therefore, it is often said: Help yourself, Heaven will help you! This explains why, given how many opponents of Americanism have become so numerous in recent times, we must be very careful with regard to the strict application of the electoral laws in matters of ballots counting, monitoring, presence of both parties during the counting process, and all. It is true that the past is the past. But we must always avoid repeating the same past errors. In other words, Republicans in Congress must not have fear of impeachment rumors making them believe they would be subject to losing both Senate and Congress chambers. In this sense, if the latter have become cowards and wet hens to believe, it is that they are not lawyers worthy of being the representatives of the people in their respective states.

These Republicans in question must retain good memories to remember that Russia-Russia, Ukraine, and China COVID-19 were not true while Trump was quite calumniated and trapped. Although we lost both the Senate and Congress.

What about currently speaking concerning Biden's shenanigans deals with Russia, Ukraine, China, Romania to name a few, when in the eyes of everybody the cat is out of the bag? How to have fear of losing the fight when everything is quite clear crystal with palpable and indisputable evidence by bankers' checks and key eyewitnesses!? Also, they must avoid wasting time uniquely and simply on Biden's scandal of corruption in concert with his favorite partner and adorable son Hunter while there is still nuance in laws that are lame and pending in terms of their application and good functioning in matters of elections. Don't they deserve to be reviewed and corrected?

By way of conclusion, it would be a fatal error on our part not to allude in this wasteful debate within the framework leading to this impeachment, which still lasts, repeating the other. It is to say, from midday to midnight, while the facts are there and that also the evidence is crystal clear to everyone's eyes, even a novice in matters of law and crime against the sovereignty and security of the country, UNITED STATES OF AMERICA considered as THE MASTERY OF THE PLANET ON EARTH!

For this, noting the weakness and the wind of disagreement which have often existed, and this, still currently between the Republicans themselves, compared to the Democrats devoting themselves to defending their party with teeth and nails even when found guilty in flagrante delicto. From this, we deduce that the ripe BANANA is suchly soft that it has never been right even with rotten teeth! This is the best way we can ourselves arrogate with the right, for the full comprehension of our readers to describe this impeachment pitting the Republicans versus the Democrats, more precisely President Joe Biden and his family.

Although ultra sine qua non, this impeachment, however, it is also important to underline why those raconteurs and nonsense arguments, when it is no longer a secret for anyone that currently speaking, the country is really going through an acute crisis, not to say in peril with all kinds of problems? With all these testimonies and proofs on hands, can it be difficult for Republicans to see that the cat is out of the bag? If so, why take from midday to midnight to vote if yes or no President Biden is guilty? When we already know that the Democrats being in majority in the Senate will never accept Joe Biden be liquidated and collapsed!

By the way, to kill time, many so-called congressmen radical-left liberals have had the audacity to make Donald Trump responsible for such an impeachment. But it's ultra false and exaggerated thinking that way! Trump already knew although tides and storms he will win in apotheosis on November 5, 2024! We are less a year from the D day, while Trump is up by 11 points over Sleepy Joe Biden! Why encourage an impeachment against him?

In contrast, Trump dreams every night is to masterfully beat Biden again, but this time, by a margin super solidified speaking where even if they would intend to operate heavy shenanigans as they did in 2020 in Pennsylvania that Trump will not be affected! According to a MAGA's supporter that we might trust, in regard of Biden's impeachment, Trump would have said: if I believe that my adversary is already defeated, how to want an impeachment for this guy?

Anyway, for your memory and your followers, I want to prove to the American people that I still can do it again in 2024 and this is similar to Ronald Reagan's style 1984. Such would seem a clear answer of Donald to a Republican reporter.

In this context, supporters of the Americanism Revolution having as their principal leader Donald Trump must start to sort the seeds well today even before planting them for a very correct harvest on November 5, 2024, of which nothing will be able to disturb the clarity of such a victory in apotheosis as would not have been the case in 2020. Also, it's not a small task choosing as a symbol of our monetary effigy, namely: IN GOD WE TRUST. But this testifies to a great belief on the part of the United States and Americans to consider God as their compass. This will also be said that this same supreme being owes a royalty of responsibility towards this country in question which recognizes in him the master power being able to redeem and deliver the United States from bad people's hands.

However, despite all, these devils tried by all means, acting in good Saint Thomas to not respect and believe in the Beyond, choosing someone to lead the country. Their memory is quite short to ignore this very meaningful thought, namely: one can always hit the game, but not the player. After more than forty years, they still don't take into account that this player in question, (DONALD TRUMP) has his roots deep and numerous. They are very difficult to be completely uprooted. But however, in case that happens, they will grow back shortly.

In this context, we are inclined to let them well assimilate that everything they can't understand remains a mystery beyond their ability. Therefore, the question that more than one should ask, do they really want to be aware of the truth? If so, they should take into account several signs of events that occurred during this last time, testifying and showing that Donald Trump is not alone! Trump is seconded and guided by an invisible power of which he is personally unaware!

Why such a rag burned between Congressman Gaetz and ex-speaker McCarthy, wwhen we all know that Gaetz remains a fervent supporter of Donald Trump? It was not without reason we even wanted him to be quid as much as the Trumpets were angry at his decision to create panic in the lower house causing the upheaval of McCarthy as speaker. Thus everyone thought that everything had been done to Donald Trump's Disadvantage, but not at all!

Therefore, as well formulated above: everything we do not understand is a mystery and exceeds our capacity as being simply human beings. But we refuse to know that we are all really little on earth. We are like the roses that grow on street corners. However, instead of kneeling before him, we often want to thwart his divine will to be his adversary and propose to fight from the mouth to the nails against his desire. But again, God had his disposal!

All this it is to say again that this altercation occurred for reasons that the reason itself can't explain because after only a week as speaker, it seems that the majority of the Republicans are convinced that the new Speaker is about to well respect the partition of Republican music. It is a sign of foretaste showing that he continues on this same path, he will open the door wide for Donald Trump leading to a trifecta in 2025, which will also allow the majority to govern well, unlike 2020.

According to some sources that we can trust, given that all hope is lost for DeSantis in 2024 after tending to betray Trump, Johnson attracts numerous Republicans who seem not to mind that he will be a future impending replacement for Donald Trump in cases where everything cooks well between him and the latter. They do insist again: in cases nothing would disturb the harmony and clarity of this wonderful beginning. In all this, we do not believe that the rebellion of the Democrats goes further than that because Hillary Clinton and Donna Brazile, two close ultra-activist liberals, have just sounded the alarm cry. In the eyes of the Democratic Party, and we quote: "Since our entire life in matters of political movements, we never experienced such a similar phenomenal movement, MAGA."

So such an unexpected message from the two headquarters of the party seems to spread fear and terror among the liberal Democrats, making them know that they risk losing 31 seats in the lower house if the crisis of all kinds to which they are confronted continues.

In this sense, the latter must know that a party without historic memory is a party without hope. They must not lose the good memory to remember that history, whether from a political or biblical point of view, is only an endless beginning. This takes us back to the Old Testament of Exodus chapter 14 verses 19 to 31! What did happen when the Israelites were about to cross the Red Sea? God ordered Moses to divide the sea in two ways to facilitate free access to his people, which was well done. But as for the Egyptians who followed the people of God to kill the latter, once they arrived for the crossing, the Red Sea erupted and became deeper because The Lord ordered Moses to act in the opposite direction.

As a result, all these wicked and Egyptian enemies perished. Then to all those who want to thwart the will of God, trying to destroy the one he has chosen to M-A-G-A, will be mounted and shipwrecked in the open sea, just like the Egyptians, to never resurface because the wrath of God will make them pay their boldness and lack of respect for the Supreme Being. So, the message is crystal clear. Thus, word to the wise, hello! hello!

In this sense, we believe that God is someone who's just and real, while never alternating his promises to those who respect and adore him. But nevertheless, given how we have become mad to detach ourselves from sacred principles and laws coming from divinity by which, we below must submit. Instead, we preferably forget, to repeat after the other that we are nothing, but really few things, not to say roses growing around the corner of the streets. We also ignore that we are only simple bodies! However, bodies without heads are good for nothing for bodies being below the heads! In other words, the body is always dependent on the head for normal functioning. It cannot survive without the power above, which is the brain!

However, engulfing in this visible world to detach ourselves from sacred principles and laws coming from divinity by which we are currently living. In this sense, our intuition leads us in error, that of being like SAINT THOMAS to only believe when we see. Thus, after so many sad events that have happened recently, don't they see that Donald Trump is the one called for by this indivisible being we are talking about to get the nation out of such an embarrassment of all kinds it is facing actually? Despite all this, do they still want to thwart divine will? Don't they also realize that every time they try to persecute and unjustly imprison Donald Trump, this fearsome Americanophile has become more and ultra-popular? Don't they have a good memory to recognize that they are reliving a similar story of what happened between the people of Israel and those of Egypt on the Red Sea (Exodus 14: 19-31)?

If memory no longer fails them, they must be able to see this brace of similarity existing between then and today where they must stop having a tendency to collapse and toast Trump! Acting that way is purely and fervently setting yourselves up as tough adversaries to refute on the wrong foot the willingness of the one you cannot neither see nor touch making the choice of Donald Trump not only to lead the United States but also to bring it back to safety.

You must also note that today, this same infallible God is going to allow Donald J. Trump to respect his commitments to rescue us by lifting our financial burdens. To do so, Trump, the very next day after swearing in, will set to work in concert with the congress anytime analyzing mutually the situation of gravity that we are crossing to once for all correct together the catastrophic blunders left by Joe Biden's liberal and careless administration. Because even Democrats elected must know that with Biden we inherited a bad souvenir of the latter.

Without wanting to be quite severe towards him, we are inclined to recognize that it requires a lot of determination and sacrifice, to correct this incurable wound that President Biden gave us as a gift during his four years in office. Also, there are rumors regarding Trump's attitude leading as a dictator, once swearing in 2025. In this nonsense opinion, we would have urged and exhorted the people to put the diatribes of those everlasting oligarchs' opponents away. Their only objective dating since 2017 has not changed, which is collapsing Trump because they don't ever want him, as an outsider, to make big history! That's why they never stop harassing him and accusing him of all the sins of the world.

Therefore, contrary to these unfounded criticisms coming from this bitterness and jealousy so-called leaders of the people, among whom are Hillary Clinton and Chris Christie to name only these two. They make the American people believe that with Donald Trump in power in 2025, it is the great return to the hunt for all those who were and are still against him. Unfortunately, the message does not move even an inch with the firm willingness of voters who already made up their mind and decide to vote in droves for Trump. Once again, their message for Hillary, Big Chris Christie is crystal clear: we are tired of your nonsense shenanigans. These are all words of wind that the wind carries and which blow before our door.

So, alluding from this thought pre-classic century of Francois de Villon (French writer) is to make professional swindlers know that the message emanating from THE VOX POPULI, VOX DEI will no longer change.

They are all, Blacks, Whites, Latinos, Asians, Jews, etc., to understand that in a country which is in danger of this kind, Donald J. Trump is the only solution to remedy this situation. We declare all that once arrived in power on January 20, 2025, we, the voice of the voiceless, feel confident and optimistic to consistently once again declare that nothing is impossible for Donald Trump.

He won't be on his first try. Trump is used to dealing with it. We don't caress any sign of doubt through our intuition and belief that with Trump back in the White House on January 20, 2025, we'll no longer walk with our heads down, but with our hearts held high. We will no longer be unhappy, but happy. We will never again be the tail, but the head. He simply asks us to continue to live with hope, faith, and love. Because of the immeasurable love and protection you have always testified towards me, I assume the responsibility to consider myself as the Architect of your future destiny by exhausting you to believe that although through tides and storms, Donald Trump will be capable of keeping all his promises to the American people, that of relieving their life which oftentimes is flouted and mistreated.

Fellow compatriots, trust him! So, with his skills, love, faith, conscience, professionalism, and his willingness to do things right, contrary to what devils already predicted that will happen, know once for all that is cries of despair and defeat already conceded by Trump's enemies.

Don't worry about speculations and questions of Hitler and others. It's not without reason that seeing them start rising up against each other!

Observe well! Even before they judge and condemn Donald Trump, they will already be under the locks of the one by whom Trump has been guided to resurface and regain control of the White House in good and proper form in 2025. However, given they are saturated by evils, they consistently continue acting in Saint Thomas to only believe until they see crystal clear.

Having said so, it is to prove how these rebellious oligarchs and sellers of the country refuse to believe in the power of the highest! It's difficult for them to appeal to memory and history to remember that Donald Trump is already chosen by the one we don't know and cannot see to guide the United States and Israel towards peace and progress.

Don't be afraid! Trust in him! He's the one to whom I give the command. Be confident and faithful. Trump will put us back on our two military feet and nudge us to walk in the right direction so that together we will possess the full power to make AMERICA GREAT AGAIN.

MR. 1WONDERFUL1

Fluent in English, French, Spanish.

Highly Independent thinking and creating.

Strong speaking and writing skills.

Singer and music composer.

Responsible, professional, pleasant and personable.

Nicolas Ismael was born in Port-au-Prince, Haiti at midday under the tree called, Bois-d'homme (Wood Man). Without doubt, the roots of Bois-d'homme incarnated in him a gift of creativity, a sense of humor and inspiration making him easier to analyze and comment on events. Already, from his young age, such a gift was noticed through radio broadcasting due to his charismatic style.

Nicolas created a following before having immigrated to the USA.

Shortly after arriving in New York, while watching a television show on CBS, he quickly noticed that the host of the show repeatedly used throughout this program the word, Wonderful!

Since French is Ismael's official language, the latter referred himself to his English/French dictionary to find the meaning of the word in question, which means, "Merveilleux." Since then, all his audience knows him as Mr 1wonderful1.

Mr.1wonderful1 is someone widely respected for his sense of humor and sympathy for human kind.

Additionally, his non-biased reporting of news, sport segments and community events for his radio show on WNWK, WEVD, WNJR, including comments and editorials for many local Newspapers in Brooklyn NY qualified him as a successful media personality.

Mr 1wonderful1 hosts community events as Master of Ceremonies. He also organizes festivals with Caribbean and Latino bands and media.

Mr.1wonderful1's work as a Broadcaster, has put him in touch with many up and coming. Artists and musical bands, which lead him to a career as a Promoter. Meanwhile, his love for music laid the groundwork to compose several arrangements that are based on people's daily lifestyle, namely: emotional issues such as love, racism, passion that you should be able to listen to soon on Mr 1wonderful1 YouTube.

The style varies from Rock and Roll, R&B to Romantic love songs such: Happy birthday, Be on the move, Surprise meeting, True love, Miss Picky, New York New York, Boogie Woogie Jazz and Desire Dream encompass his talents.

Mr. 1wonderful1 latest creative achievement is actually written two marvelous long short stories about politics and romance.

The first one, HIGHER RESOLUTION VS GEOPOLITICAL RISKS, is inspired by his love and his patriotism for his country, USA.

As a brainseller following his business political course for a long period of time, I said to myself, why not shedding the light for those whose knowledge is quite limited to understand how much this hard working billionaire always wants the United States to remain the greatest on earth. Especially when he has never stopped reiterating:

America First! However, it's really deplorable that many people have oftentimes misinterpreted his concept and admiration for this nation, instead nicknamed Trump racist.

The second book having for title: IS LOVE BLIND?

The story takes me back to my teenage years in Haiti where my cousin triumphs over many difficult odds to win the heart of a beautiful young woman. It is a true story that reveals funny segments, lies, sex, drama, voodoo, reli- gion and, most of all, a happy ending despite all of the tides and storms endured during its beginnings and throughout its existence.

Made in the USA
Middletown, DE
08 April 2024

52590945R00106